Joe

Joe's Journey

Joseph Soukup vs. The State of Nebraska

Joseph Soukup
Rebecca Schmieding Shacklett
Dawna Prietauer

Infusionmedia
P U B L I S H I N G
Lincoln, Nebraska

INFUSIONMEDIA PUBLISHING INC.
140 North 8th Street
205 The Apothecary
Lincoln, NE 68508-1358
Voice/Fax: 402-477-2065
Email: info@infusionmediapublishing.com

Printed in the United States.

10 9 8 7 6 5 4 3 2 1

ISBN 0-9718677-6-3

Cover photography by Rebecca Schmieding Shacklett.

Table of Contents

Notes to the Reader

JOSEPH Soukup is quick to call this effort a work of "fiction." The information and views in this account are those of Joe's and are a reflection of his memories and perceptions. Whenever possible, verbatim text from official documents has been included but names of doctors and other staff have been assigned initials in hospital and social service records. The reader will note inconsistencies not only in Joe's memory of these events, but also in the statements of professionals in Nebraska institutions and agencies. The Lincoln State Hospital (now the Lincoln Regional Center) was no different than other large institutions in relying on the staff interpretation of behavior as it supports their views of the role "patient." What indeed is behavior we call "assertive" vs. "stubborn"? And will behavior be differently assessed if demonstrated by a staff person or a patient?

In collaborating on this work, Joe was surprised and saddened to hear some of the statements made in progress notes and evaluations by doctors and other State Hospital staff. Many of the accusations about his behavior are statements he can neither prove nor disprove. It appears these statements, once made, become "facts" in each subsequent document. He is repeatedly called a liar and thief but there is little documentation of events that support these labels. Joe believes these statements to be untrue; he also realizes the less powerful position he speaks from when other voices are doctors and professionals. His commitment is to tell this story in all honesty. He does not want anything excluded from the reader even if it paints him in a negative light.

Rebecca Schmieding Shacklett is a registered nurse who holds a master of education degree and a master of forensic science degree. She worked at the Lincoln Regional Center from 1969 through 1974. Joe was a patient in the same building for a short time in 1971, so their paths crossed but neither remembers the other! Some of the individuals mentioned are known to both Joe and Rebecca; statements we make are in no way intended to disparage these professionals or their work in the mental health field. We are writing as we look back over fifty years. Much has changed in the field, and our hopes with this document are that the reader understands both the history and the values of mental health services during these years.

Dawna Prietauer is an associate of applied science degree graduate of the Human Services Program at Southeast Community College. She is a Certified Compulsive Gambling Counselor and a Provisional Licensed Alcohol and Drug Counselor. Dawna completed many of the initial interviews and did background research for this story.

Joe's Journey

JOE Soukup is an unlikely hero in the narrative of Nebraska's mental health treatment history. Joe, held illegally for four years in the Lincoln State Hospital, now lives independently on a trust fund established by the Nebraska Unicameral in 1981. It was not money easily extracted from the state. Joe's case went to the State Claims committee for four consecutive years before he was awarded relief. Joe has asked that this book be called "Joe's Journey."

This is a tale not unlike current news exposés; foster children lost for days or years in systems both overworked and undersupervised. It is a story that contains some malice but much more ineptitude. It is the story of a physical giant, as David, to a much bigger Goliath, the State of Nebraska.

This is also the story of the effects of "growing up" in institutions. It is a tale of lost identity, of no longer being able to tell someone's original "problem" from the personality created by institutionalization.

As a child in the '40s and '50s, Joe loved to pretend he was cowboy hero Roy Rogers to his sister's Dale Evans. Later he loved playing chess, testing in the normal range of IQ. He was eager to please others and valued human interaction above material gain. Fifteen years later, after shock treatment and being a "guinea pig" for LSD experiments, a very different adult walked away from the grounds of the State Hospital at Folsom and Van Dorn Streets in Lincoln, Nebraska. How much is the Joe of today similar to the one who was sent to "reform school" at age ten? We'll never know for sure because most of the medical records have been lost. Joe purchased copies of his chart for his twelve-year, three-month, fifteen-day, eight-hour and forty-seven-minute stay with the state. The cost was twenty cents per sheet. Only thirty-two sheets of paper could be found.

Much of this story relies on Joe's memory of his early years. He admits a great deal has been lost in his recollections of the time. He contributes this memory problem to over 150 shock treatments (electroconvulsive therapy). There is no proof of these treatments although we know they were common at the time. That the State Hospital (now named the Lincoln Regional Center) gave patients LSD as experimental psychopharmacology is undisputed. The hospital acknowledges that at least one dose of intravenous LSD was given to Joe, but he recalls receiving at least three doses of the drug. And that Joe was sterilized also relies on his vivid recall of the events of that day.

This document will explore Joe's early history, the scope of his institutional stays, his fight for justice, and his life as he lives it today.

Joe's Early Life
According to Joe

JOE was born at 6:30 in the evening on January 6, 1943, to Joseph Soukup and Helen Francis at Lutheran Hospital in Omaha, Nebraska. His first ten years were spent in a four-bedroom, red-brick home at 502 North 20th Street in Omaha. Joe's sister Pat was born on December 20, 1944. Joe's memories of his first ten years are spotty; he believes this is a long-term effect of all the shock treatments. It is important to remember that Joe was removed from his home at age ten. Childhood memories for all of us at this early age are more a mosaic than a narrative. And most of us have some degree of continuing contact with nuclear and extended family that includes stories, traditions and photographs. Joe, at age ten, had none of these.

Joe does remember the day his father brought home their first black-and-white television set. It received only the three Omaha stations and not always with the best reception. Of course, this was long before modern cable or satellite service. The family would watch wrestling on the seven-inch screen on Saturdays. Weekdays were for *Howdy Dowdy* which was on at 3:30 p.m. after school. Joe remembers his father doing repair work around the house, and by age five, Joe was pleased to carry his father's tool box for these projects. Joe's mother loved to sing and would follow along with the radio on top of the refrigerator whenever the "Tennessee Waltz" or the music of Patty Page came on.

Like many moms of the '40s and '50s, Helen was a stay-at-home mom and "housewife." She was five feet, two inches tall, a heavyset brunette with hazel eyes (which Joe inherited). Helen wore her hair shoulder-length and usually wore housedresses, never slacks. Macaroni and cheese, hamburger steaks and, still Joe's favorite, liver and onions were among Helen's staples for the family. Joe's mom would often take him with her to the grocery store and let him push the cart. Joe's dad, Joe Sr., worked for a local cab company, driving a limousine to and from the airport. He also was a supervisor for the company and worked at the office, usually the evening and night shifts. He was a tall, "solid" man of six feet, two inches who drank socially but never to excess. His dad would come home after working all night, go upstairs to a part of the house that was off limits to the kids, and sleep for four or five hours before getting up to spend the day with his family.

A favorite family spot was Bud and Joe's Café at 18th and Chicago Street in Omaha. The favorite menu item: hamburgers. The Café would sell leftover buns at 10 p.m., a bargain for a family with limited income.

Joe's Irish mother and Bohemian father took their children to St. John's Catholic Church and were "quite religious." Joe attended parochial school for the first three grades and recalls liking school and felt he fit in just fine. Joe remembers learning values of honesty and being trustworthy. They were just starting on lessons in good manners when he was removed from the home. Joe doesn't ever recall his parents arguing. If they had private things to talk about, they went into a room and shut the door to discuss them.

Joe remembers only one relative, his mother's brother Ray. Uncle Ray would visit frequently and these visits usually involved a quarter each for his nephew and niece. The Rexall Drug Store and Plotkin's Grocery Store across the street from Joe's home would then become the site for obtaining as much penny candy as twenty-five cents would allow. In those days, "a kid could buy a lot of penny candy for a quarter." Another sign of the standard of living at the time was the amount left by the tooth fairy for each lost tooth: Ten cents! An ice cream truck, complete with bell, was another source of pleasure in Joe's early life.

Joe does not recall meeting any grandparents or other relatives. He did not know until many years later that his father had been married before and had six other children.

Despite many good memories, Joe does remember his mother's stash of fifths of vodka, hidden in every room in the house. She would drink all day, everyday, usually drinking out of a different bottle everywhere she would go throughout the house. His father kept their marriage together and did not know how to handle the problem or did not realize how serious it had become. Joe does not remember the details, but does know that his mom died at age twenty-nine. Her death certificate lists the cause of death as "alcoholism resulting in malnutrition." All he remembers of that day, April 17, 1953, is his father came and told him that "Mom's gone." Despite attending the funeral, Joe didn't know quite what that meant until about two weeks later when the reality finally sunk in that mom would not be coming home.

Joe Sr. became ill shortly after this, suffering from a painful cyst on his neck. Joe can remember visiting him in the hospital, and his dad would have half of his face covered with a bandage. Joe was there when the cancerous cyst on his dad's face burst. He knows his father experienced a great deal of pain before his death. Joseph Soukup died on August 20, 1956, at age fifty-six. The cause of death was listed as "Squamous cell CA (cancer) of lips with widespread metastasis to neck."

By 1952 at age nine, Joe had already come to the attention of Omaha authorities, originally for curfew violations. He was removed from his parents' home and placed in the Riverview Home, a group home in Omaha. But Joe would not "stay put" and continued to run home. Joe's father would refuse to return Joe to the authorities of Riverview Home. He was upset with the state for splitting his family apart and was resentful that Joe could not stay at home. In October 1952, the Douglas County Juvenile Court filed a petition stating that Joe was a delinquent. With an alcoholic mother and a father who worked the night shift, Joe and his sister Pat were found to be neglected and without proper parental supervision. Both children were placed in the custody of the Catholic Charities in Douglas County, Omaha, Nebraska. Pat went to the St. James Orphanage and Joe was sent to the Boys' Training School in Kearney, Nebraska. Both were "temporary" placements pending his mother's recovery or death. Joe recalls the day this decision was made. He was waiting outside the courtroom and his father came out and told him he was being sent to Kearney.

Joe entered the Boys' Training School on December 31, 1953. He scored in the average range on IQ tests. About 100 delinquent boys were in the Kearney program, but Joe, as tall as an eighteen-year-old, was the youngest. Despite his young age, Joe says he received "no special treatment." He attended classes and did chores, including washing dishes, yard work, and he even learned how to darn socks with a light bulb stuck inside. One existing document stated, "Joe's social adjustment relationships were excellent and he is a well poised youth." He was rated average in willingness, cooperation, ability, and occupational training. However, discipline is one thing Joe remembers quite well about Kearney and he often jokes that he was on a first-name basis with a razor strap during his time there.

In 1956, Joe was transferred to Father Flannagan's Boys Town in Omaha, Nebraska, an orphanage made famous in the 1938 movie *Boys Town* and known for the slogan, "He's not heavy, he's my brother." Apparently Joe was "too heavy," because in February of 1967, Boys Town wrote back to Kearney, saying Joe had lots of problems in their facility; he was untruthful, had fantasies, and told lies. They stated that Joe had been "examined" and there was a possibility of organic brain damage. Kearney did not want Joe back, so they wrote the Lincoln State Hospital, stating he was having trouble in Boys Town, he had made little progress at Kearney and could no longer benefit from the Kearney Boys' Training School. Now all this is in direct conflict with Kearney's assessment of Joe when they were trying to "unload him" to Boys Town! And all this transferring took place with no guardian *ad lidum*, no independent neurological or psychiatric examination, and no court proceedings to ensure Joe's rights. In an

October 29, 1977, article in the Grand Island newspaper, Joe recalls no hearing "unless they held a mental health board hearing in the car between Omaha and Lincoln."

Omaha Social Services View

Now, contrast Joe's memories with this social services summary completed at the time of his admission to Kearney. This social history was one of the few documents that survived (author comments in italics, all other text in quotes is verbatim; this form will be followed throughout the book):

Birth Date: 1-6-43-(Verified)
CountyRes.: Douglas
Address: Boys' Training School
Parents: Joseph Sloukup [sic], Sr.
              502 North 20 Street
              Omaha, Nebraska
              Helen Sullivan Soukup
              deceased.

WORKER
R.A.
DATE OF SOCIAL SUMMARY
January 27, 1954

REFERRAL
In a letter dated January 1, 1954 we were asked by Mr. M. W., Superintendent of the Boys' Training School, to furnish a social history on Joseph Soukup, who was admitted to the Boys' Training School December 31, 1953. The information for this history was obtained from records from Catholic Charities and the Juvenile Court: Mr. Soukup refused to give any information because he was not in agreement with the action of Catholic Charities or the Court, and was planning to hire an attorney to have his boy released from the Boys' Training School.

FAMILY BACKGROUND
Father: Joseph Soukup, Sr. was born February 24, 1900 in Brainard, Nebraska. He is presently employed as a limousine drive [sic] for the Municipal Air Port Limousine Service; his weekly salary will average $70. He is of Bohemian extraction, and a member of the Catholic Church; however, his attendance is irregular. He has received eight grades of education.

Mother: Helen Sullivan Soukup was born December 25, 1922 at Sidney, Nebraska. She was of Irish extraction, and was a member of the Protestant faith. She had received eight grades of education. Mrs. Soukup died of cancer on April 17, 1953.

Sister: Patricia Soukup was born December 20, 1944 in Omaha, Nebraska. On August 19, 1953 the Douglas County Juvenile Court took custody of Patricia and placed the supervision of her with Catholic Charities; she was placed in St. James Orphanage, where she still resides.

Religion: Mr. Soukup is a member of the Catholic Church, but Mrs. Soukup was of the Protestant faith. Joseph, Jr. has not been baptized or confirmed but did attend the Catholic Church regularly and had attended Catholic grade school.

Marital History: Mr. Soukup was married to Enid Johnson December 11, 1923, and was divorced from her September 30, 1933. The worker at Catholic Charities stated that he deserted his first wife and six children. Mr. Soukup married Helen Sullivan July 28, 1941 in Omaha, Nebraska, this marriage being terminated by the death of Mrs. Soukup April 17, 1953.

FAMILY ATTITUDES AND BEHAVIOR

From other agency records it would appear that the Soukup family was hampered by a great many emotional conflicts. Mr. Soukup was 22 years Mrs. Soukup's senior, which could have some bearing on her immaturity and maladjustment. Mrs. Soukup was an alcoholic, and it was not uncommon for Joe and his sister to come home from school and find the mother in an alcoholic stupor. When the mother was in this condition Joe's sister Patricia would make up stories to cover up the real nature of the mother's immobility.

Mr. Soukup is a hostile, acting out person, who cannot assume his responsibility for the situation of his children. He is quite hostile toward Catholic Charities and the Juvenile Court for "breaking up his home," and has hired an attorney to secure the release of Joe from the Boys' Training School.

Mr. Soukup is employed at night, and the Court worker informed this worker that there were many nights when the children were home by themselves. Attempts were made to obtain the services of a housekeeper, but the two that were hired quit because they could not put up with the filth in the home. Mr. Soukup complained about the methods used in taking his children from him, and stated that they should have helped him keep the home together instead of tearing it down; however, Mr. Soukup would not cooperate with the agencies in working out a livable arrangement for the children in the home.

The Soukups are occupying a six-room duplex at 502 North 20th Street. This neighborhood consists mainly of apartments, multiple dwelling and duplexes. Standards of living in this neighborhood are below the average neighborhood in the city, and family life is hindered by the characteristics and behavior of the entire neighborhood.

BOY'S HISTORY

Joseph, Jr. was born January 6, 1943 in Omaha, Nebraska; the birth was a difficult one, and was an instrument delivery. Joseph was a large baby and grew at a rapid rate, being much larger than his peers. He has large hands and feet, which were the source of a lot of criticism from the other children and his parents. The boy has been told by his parents that he was peculiar looking and awkward. Many nights he would return from school in an anxiety state, asking his mother, "I'm not funny looking, am I?" (*Joe does not remember his parents ever saying anything of this nature to him.*)

Joseph's behavior has shown a great deal of emotional conflict and he is not able to form a close relationship with people. In his fantasy world he would always identify with the people that to him were peculiar and not like the average person. He enjoyed attending movies in which the main character was peculiar, with the other actors in the movie teasing and making fun of the peculiar person.

Dr. G. L. had contact with Joe in June of 1951 at the University of Nebraska Dispensary, and recently Dr. B. had contact with him while Joe was hospitalized in the Psychiatric Section of St. Joseph's Hospital (*Joe does not remember this*). Dr. B. tentatively diagnosed Joe as a character disorder, and described the boy as living half way between a fantasy world and the psychotic condition of hallucinations. Before being placed in the Psychiatric Section of the St. Joseph Hospital in July of 1953, Joe had called the case supervisor at Catholic Charities stating that he was frightened and wanted help. He told the case supervisor that there wer [sic] about a dozen men in the home, some of them had their heads cut off and some of them didn't.

Joseph fell prey to sexual perverts five or six months ago, and was the passive recipient of these perversions. He did not show any anxiety over these acts, but became very upset when he was not rewarded with money as the perverts had promised him. We feel that this boy is starved for attention, and his sexual behavior is his method of being able to give something to somebody in return for money, which to him probably represents affection.

While living in the home Joe shared a bed with his sister, and the worker at Catholic Charities stated that there was some indication of sex play between them (*"Absolutely not true," according to Joe*). This boy's mental health has been damaged considerably, and while at the Boys' Training

School he should be referred to Dr. G. L. as soon as possible.

School and Psychological Report: Joseph had attended the second grade at St. John's School, and before his trouble was taking the third grade work at Central Grade School. A report from St. John's indicated that his attendance was poor (*Joe says he was there everyday*), scholarship poor, and citizenship good. It was further stated that while in the classroom he used every means possible to gain attention, and that he was void of ability to do any abstract thinking. The Stanford Binet Tests of Intelligence, Terman-Merrill Revision, Form L, was administered September 9, 1953, by F. W., and Joe was assigned an IQ of 98, with a mental age of 9 years, 8 months.

JUVENILE COURT RECORD:

2-18-52 – Joseph was referred to the Juvenile Court for curfew violation; the boy was released to his father on the promise that closer supervisions would be given. (*Curfew violations are "status offenses," offenses that apply only to juveniles.*)

7-16-52 – Joe was referred to the Juvenile Court for taking an undisclosed amount of money from a news stand in the down town area (*Joe does not recall this*); he was placed in Riverview Home, and while there had many episodes of running away.

The last time he ran away the father refused to return him.

7-24-53 – Catholic Charities, who had been working with Joseph and the family, made a formal complaint to the Juvenile Court that Joseph and his sister Patricia were neglected and were without proper parental supervision. On 8-19-53 the Juvenile Court took custody of Joe and his sister, placing their supervision with Catholic Charities. Patricia was placed in St. James but Joseph was refused admittance because of his behavior. Catholic Charities attempted to complete a placement for Joe at Boys Town, but they were unable to follow through with this plan because Boys Town did not offer schooling under the fourth grade, so he was placed in Riverview Home. During his stay at Riverview Home the boy again had many episodes of running away, and was maladjusted in his school placement at Bancroft. Mr. Soukup failed to cooperate with the authorities, and after Joseph's first runaway refused to return him to Riverview Home. Catholic Charities and the Juvenile Court felt that Joseph would receive more protection if he were placed in the Boys' Training School at Kearney, and the Juvenile Court committed him to the Boys' Training School, he being received at the Boys' Training School December 31, 1953.

Boys' Training School at Kearney Report

Joe was taken from Omaha to the Boys' Training School at Kearney, Nebraska, a two-hour trip in a state car that came to get him. The school was located 2.5 miles outside of town and over 125 miles from Omaha, making the likelihood of a successful "elopement" slim.

An intake summary was completed on April 19, 1954, at the Boys' Training School at Kearney Nebraska, and provides a third view of Joe's childhood. Joe's Official Commitment was listed as "Delinquency" and the Act Committed: "Trouble in School." The body of the document is labeled: "Boy's statement regarding delinquency, his family, etc.":

1. PREVIOUS RECORD: None.
2. PRESENT OFFENSE:
    A. According to Joe he has never been actively involved in any law violation and was at a loss to explain his commitment to this institution. He stated his father received a notice they were to report for a court hearing on December 18, 1953 at one o'clock. A discussion was held and he was committed to this institution. Joe was asked concerning the perversion attacks on himself and related several offenses, twelve in all as he recalled, and in only one instance was he involved more than once with the same man. He stated the first offense took place on January 7th, 1952. He was walking home and when passing an alley was shoved into the alley by a Mr. P. who then committed an act of sodomy against the boy. Joe also stated, Mr. P. testified against him at the hearing. He stated that he had never at anytime had intercourse or sexual relations of any type with his sister.
    B. Summary of Impressions:
        It is quite difficult to summarize this boy. He has made considerable change for the better since entering the institution but is known to be very untruthful. At the first interview with the boy he told the writer he saw "visions", a woman and two men. He did not know who they were as he had never been able to see their faces clearly.
        However, at a later interview he stated he no longer saw these visions and felt it was because he was no longer frightened. In his home he was required to sleep alone on the second floor of the home, while his father and sister had bedrooms on the lower floor. Joe is very eager for attention and affection and it is

believed his "fantastic tales" seem to give him the prestige he so desires. He is quite effeminate in his actions and has little interest in the activities usual in boys of this age.

3. SOCIAL HISTORY:

A. Family Background:

    a) Father: Jess Soukup, age 54, lives at 502 North 20th, Omaha. Presently he is employed by an Omaha air port as a limousine driver. According to the boy Mr. Soukup has had two years of college work. He is of Catholic faith and attends regularly. The boy is very fond of this father and stated he always tried to mind him. When it was necessary however his father would discipline him. Mr. Soukup has an even temper, does not drink to excess, and Joe said "was very good to me." He also stated "he took us to a show a couple of times and to the fair once. We had a lot of fun." Mr. Soukup likes boxing and is interested in handicraft, principally woodwork and has made several lamps. According to Joe his father went to work at 8:30 in the evening and would arrive home around five in the morning. He would remain up until the children had had breakfast.

    b) Mother: The mother, Helen Francis, died when 29 years of age. Joe stated his mother had been ill approximately nine years. He has no love or affection for his mother and stated he was never really happy until after the death of his mother. She drank a great deal in the home and he stated he and his younger sister knew her hiding places for whisky and would often find the liquor and destroy it. She was cruel to the children when drinking. He also told of following his mother and a neighbor man with whom she drank to the "Trocedero" where they would stand outside and watch her. Mrs. Soukup had a junior high school education, and at the time of her death was baptized in the Catholic Church. Even when she was alive the two children did the house work. The mother argued with them a great deal, and also with the father.

Joe told of an incident when the parents took the younger sister and left town overnight. Joe was not at home when they left and apparently no effort was made to locate him. He stated he slept on the porch (*Joe recalls this incident. He was angry with his parents and "stormed" out of the house and his family went ahead and left without him*).

    c) Brothers: None

d) Sisters: Patricia, age 9, is in the 6th grade. At the time of the interview Joe did not know her whereabouts but has learned since that she is in the St. James Orphanage and has been writing to her. The relationship is very close and she writes sweet, affectionate letters, and although the younger of the two, seems to be mothering the boy.

e) Paternal and Maternal Relatives:

It is quite impossible to obtain from Joe the actual relationship of the people he mentioned.

He states he has a grandmother, whom he called "Dubbs" who lives at Hastings, Nebraska, and whom he states drinks excessively. He knows little else concerning her. He also stated he had a grandfather named Detloff but had no further information regarding this man. He believes he has two uncles: Ray (Soukup or Detloff) who lives in Valley, Nebraska. This man has employment as a semi-truck driver. He is not married; is a member of the Catholic Church and does not drink. A second uncle Jack (Soukup or Detloff). lives in Hastings, Nebraska and is employed as a pick up truck driver. He is married and has one child. The boy stated he often saw Jack in Omaha and liked him. Jack is a member of the Catholic church. He owns his home and Joe stated he visited in this home approximately four weeks before his entrance to this institution.

An aunt Tide (Tootie) lives in Valley, Nebraska. She is married and recently lost an infant child by death. There is a second aunt, Mrs. J. C. Sullivan, believed to live in Omaha. This lady and the grandparents Detloff visited Joe at the institution (*Joe remembers being told they had come to visit him but that he was not allowed to see them; no reason for denial of the visit was given*).

B. Home and Neighborhood:

Mr. Soukup owns the two-story home in which the family resides. Each had their own bedroom. They had nice furniture, a sofa bed, and were always well clothed. The father did the laundry and cooking, and according to the boy the step-grandmother often assisted in the housework. They have a TV set and most of the leisure time of the boy and his sister was spent in the home. A shopping district is located approximately six blocks away and a show three blocks. There were parks and playgrounds near but the two children did not frequent them, as other children made fun of them and had upon occasion beat them.

C. Personal History:
- a) Early Life: Joe was born in Omaha, Nebraska, January 6, 1943. He has always made his home in Omaha and has never traveled out of the state of Nebraska. When the mother was living his home life was very unhappy but since her death and while living with his father and sister he was very happy. He stated his Christmas presents were still at home and the grass would be very tall and need cutting.

4. Medical Record: Joe stated he had had measles but could recall no other childhood disease. He also stated he had had an appendectomy at the St. Joseph Hospital in Omaha. He is a tall boy, much taller than the average his age, and has a large frame. He is 5' 3 ½" in height and weighs 110 pounds. He has very blonde [sic] hair, and brown eyes. His ears are large and are set high on his head giving him rather an elfish look.

5. Education:
Joe has attended two schools. The St. John Parochial and the Central Grade School. He prefers the Catholic school, and did much better work there. He likes school and enjoys both arithmetic and spelling. Joe expressed the desire to go through high school and college.

6. Employment:
He had for two months prior to his admission to this institution been selling papers. He has had no other employment.

7. Religion:
He is a member of the Catholic Church and enjoys any participation in church. He has been baptized and communed (*Joe's confirmation name was "Aloyous" after Boys Town's Father Flanagan*).

8. Interests and Activities:
Joe's reading activity is limited but he does occasionally enjoy reading one of the Hardy boy [sic] series. He has never had a hobby and stated he did not intend to ever have one. He enjoys classical music and would like to play a drum. Main activity has been cowboy games and foot racing.
When released he wishes to return to his father and attend school.

Comments

We now have three views of Joe's early life notable for their inconsistencies and some factual inaccuracies. For instance, Joe's mother died of alcoholism, not cancer as the Kearney report states.

Phillip Ferguson, Ph.D., in his work *Abandoned to their Fate*, discusses the history of perceptions of those with mental illness or development disabilities. It would appear these perceptions of failure were consciously or unconsciously in operation by the service providers of the day. The Perception of Failure has three sub-groups of "failure" and one can see Joe's case in each.

Aesthetic Failure

The first is "aesthetic failure," assumptions about appearance being used to diagnose disabilities; if you look odd, you must be odd. Joe was characterized in the Omaha report as a large baby, the product of a difficult labor and instrument delivery. He was immediately "trouble" for his parents by causing such a difficult birth to his mother (who goes on to become an alcoholic). Unfortunately, Joe's birth certificate does not list weight and length. Joe does not recall ever hearing about being a large baby or being a difficult delivery. Joe's rapid physical development, including his height for his age and the large size of his hands and feet, made him appear different than others, "elfin" in one report. As an adult of six feet, five inches, Joe's size and looks, coupled with his sarcastic wit, were enough to cause fear in some people upon their first meeting with him.

Moral Failure

The second failure is "moral failure," the interpretation of actions that cast a person as ethically or sexually deviant. Joe's participation at age ten in "perversion," possibly for money, labels him as a moral failure who should have run away or "beat up" the "pervert." Once these sexually related "facts" are known to the observer, the perceptions by observers are forever altered. The Kearney worker now sees Joe as "quite effeminate in his actions and has little interest in the activities usual in boys of his age." One cannot help but wonder if the worker was evaluating him on the basis of his size or his age. A ten-year-old who is as tall as some adults might look "effeminate" if one forgets the usual actions of most ten-year-old boys. Joe was one of the youngest boys at Kearney at that time, so we do not know if the worker's comment regarding "activities usual in boys of his age" refers to ten-year-olds or sixteen-year-olds.

The social services report from Omaha is incorrect in Joe's memory in regard to the family's religious life. He insists that both his parents were Catholic and attended St. John's Catholic Church. He also states he was both baptized and communed. Is it possible that some bias exists in the worker's view that allows him to accept as fact the "mixed marriage" and the lack of religious formal ties. Is it impossible to believe someone who is baptized and communed can also participate in "sexual perversions"?

Joe is adamant in regard to his relationship to his sister and denies any sexual activity with her. The Omaha report gives no evidence to support this save for the Catholic Charities statement "that there was some indication of sex play between them." Is the fact that the children were left alone a trigger for this assumption? Was this normal sibling curiosity misconstrued as deviant behavior? Without more facts, we will never know. Joe, who was there, states this was not true.

Joe's father is also cast in this moral failure. He "deserted" his wife and six children according to a worker at Catholic Charities. This statement is made with no known investigation into the facts of the first marriage, but given the official position of the Catholic Church on divorce, one can see how this event would not be seen as a positive move no matter what the cause. And marrying a woman twenty-two years his junior is what led to "immaturity and maladjustment" of Joe's mother rather than the disease of alcoholism.

Joe's father's rejection of the assistance and advice of Catholic Charities is another "moral failure." How dare he question their wisdom when they "only want what's best for his family."

Economic Failure

The third failure is "economic failure," the powerlessness that comes with the lack of resources that is the American ideal. If one examines the common belief that anyone can succeed in this country if they just work hard enough, those who are poor are obviously not only poor but also "shiftless and stupid." The criticism of the state of his family home is especially vexing to Joe. While his home was not ideal, it was certainly not the hovel portrayed by the Omaha report. In regard to the children being home alone at night, while this was not by any means a good situation, we must remember that this practice was not uncommon historically with working, lower-income persons who did not have the money for childcare. Were Joe and his sister the only children home alone in Omaha in 1952? Probably not. It is interesting to note that for most of his early life Joe's father worked at night and no social service concern was raised, even though his mother was intoxicated beyond the ability to function as a parent during that time.

Not only is Joe's family economically deprived, his entire neighborhood has, ". . . Standard of living . . . below the average neighborhood in the city, and family life is hindered by the characteristics and behavior of the entire neighborhood." This implies that not only are Joe and his family unfit, but the entire neighborhood is a disgrace.

Life at the State Hospital

"A definition is no proof."
— William Pinkney, American diplomat

The History

The Lincoln State Hospital was created by the Nebraska State Legislature through the Capitol Removal Act of 1868 and was initially called "The Nebraska Hospital for the Insane." The first building was completed and the first patient was admitted in 1870. Like most institutions of its time, it was located in a pastoral setting outside the city at Van Dorn and Folsom Streets. In a reversal of the old adage "out of sight, out of mind," mental hospitals could truly be said to be for patients who were "out of mind, out of sight."

In 1885, allegations of mistreatment prompted an investigation by a Joint Committee of the Nebraska Senate and House. Their findings included:

"1. That there is not a systematic and careful examination of patients on their entering the hospital by the Superintendent or his assistant physicians with a view to determine the extent and cause of their maladies.

"2. That there is not a systematic and thorough medical treatment of that class of patients known as curable, with a view to their speedy recovery.

"3. That there is no such complete record of treatment of patients as to their mental and physical condition as will enable anyone to judge or know whether patients are improving or not, and all records that have been shown to this committee are imperfectly kept, very defective in system, and are incomplete."

The committee recommended a complete mental and physical examination upon admission, that a psychiatrist meet with each patient at least once a week or more often, and that complete and full records be kept on each patient and their treatment. All this is ironic in terms of Joe's attempts to obtain his records 100 years later.

"Benevolent coercion" is the term used to describe the process of those in charge making decisions for people who cannot or do not recognize their need for treatment. "We're only doing what's best for you." In the hospital's early days this meant custodial shelter for thousands of Nebraskans. That changed, at least in theory, to becoming a treatment center that worked with individuals. Joe's tenure at the State Hospital occurred as this transition was taking place. It's no surprise he believes he was given very different messages from the time of his admission to the moment of his discharge.

Meals

Thirty years have not faded the memory of the culinary delight of creamed hard-boiled eggs on toast. Nor of the tough liver or the lumpy Cream of Wheat. In fact, the word "creamed" appeared paired with many institutionalized food items. Joe's vocational placement (a.k.a., unpaid work) in the kitchen was sufficient experience to encourage him to eat cold cereal for three meals a day. While the food and conditions were clean, cooking it in large "witch caldrons" was less than appetite-stimulating.

Meals were served in cafeteria areas in each building after being trucked through the tunnels from the central kitchen. Meal times were at 8:30 a.m., 12:00 noon and 4:00 p.m. Patients on each ward were escorted as groups and given thirty minutes to finish their meal. Ward staff supervised each meal and called out ward numbers when it was time for everyone to march back. The dinnerware was white crockery with a blue seal of the State of Nebraska on the rim. Utensils were marked with "P.I.," denoting "public institutions." Silverware was counted on a weekly basis.

Daily Routine

Baths and showers were observed by the staff and wards were assigned a Monday-Wednesday-Friday or Tuesday-Thursday-Saturday schedule. Every piece of clothing Joe owned was labeled "J. Soukup." Soiled clothing was collected on a weekly basis and was sent to the hospital laundry on a monthly schedule. When Joe needed new clothing or shoes, he had to obtain permission to leave the ward to visit the hospital "clothing room." At six feet, five inches, with size 17AAA shoes, it was difficult to outfit Joe from the stock of donated items. If Joe ran out of clean clothing, he had to wear hospital pajamas until what clothing he had returned from the laundry. Haircuts were given once a month at the institution barber shop and only one style, short, was approved for male patients. To shave, Joe had to check out his razor, use it within fifteen minutes, and return it to the ward staff.

When you live in an institution, life is organized to give each shift of staff specific duties. Getting out of bed at 5:30 a.m. is the responsibility of the night shift. Joe dressed, made his bed as required, and straightened his small cubicle. Then he waited for medications and breakfast as the shift change and report took place at 7:00 a.m. The day staff worked from 6:45 a.m. until 3:15 p.m and were then relieved by the evening workers. Supper, medications and a 10:00 p.m. bedtime were the responsibility of the p.m. shift. Sometimes, if the staff member was kind, patients were allowed to stay up and watch the 10:00 p.m. weather, news and sports with longtime Lincoln Channel 10 news anchor Mel Mains.

Windows all had inside screens and could only be opened with a crank; only the staff had the crank. There was no air conditioning and patients had no control of the room temperature, lights or TVs. Patients who smoked had to ask an aide for a light because patients were not allowed to carry matches or lighters.

White uniforms, name tags, and keys clearly distinguished the ward staff from the patient. Staff were referred to by "Mr., " "Mrs.," "Doctor;" patients, no matter what age, by their first name. Having keys was an important symbol of power and a clear message to patients of who was in control. A ring of keys was worn on a chain attached to the staff member's belt. These keys were always worn on the staff member's dominant side and the chain enabled a worker to unlock and relock doors without detaching the precious keys.

Joe spent about fifty percent of his years at the State Hospital in locked wards. He was housed at various times in six different buildings on thirteen different wards, including A-4, Ad-12, C-4, L-1, L-2,L-3, R-7, R-4, R-0, R-00, S-1, S-3, and S-5. When on open wards, and with little to do, Joe would often head into town, past the Humane Society, past Gooch's Mill and downtown via 9th Street. He always returned later in the day, but these unauthorized sojourns were met with a less-than-enthusiastic response from the hospital staff. Joe would lose his grounds card and be reassigned to a locked ward to work his way back up to the "privilege" of being able to leave the ward again. The first step in this process was to obtain a "green grounds card," which meant you could be off ward with a full privileges "blue card" patient.

Doctors and Nurses

Doctors were assigned to each building at the State Hospital and that building became their little kingdom. Joe believes each thought his approach to working with patients was the correct method. The hospital superintendent during Joe's stay appeared to him to manage in a "hands-off" style, accepting the word of each doctor as indisputable. One of Joe's doctors was an active alcoholic who was periodically sent to another state hospital to "dry out." Another doctor was actively psychotic and was known to stand at the window of his office and hallucinate.

Under the doctors in the pecking order were the nurses. They were the real power on the ward, influencing all that occurred for patients. Then there were the aides who had their own hierarchy of roles on the ward. The lowest in this order is, of course, the patients. Like any system built on a pyramid of power, each level must hold claim to their position by demonstrating their sphere of power, even when unnecessary.

Joe felt he was constantly being told to "keep his place," that of a lowly patient who did not know what was best for him. Even those he liked among the staff found it necessary to point out to Joe just who was in charge, and it wasn't Joe!

Conductors/Vocational Rehabilitation

Escorting individuals and groups of patients on the hospital grounds was the job of the "conductors." This group of eight staff and eight patients operated out of the third floor of the "K" building. A staff and patient pair would lead a group of patients from the ward to recreation, occupational therapy, etc., with the conductor patient as the lead and the staff conductor bringing up the rear. The "job" of patient conductor required a ground pass and was limited to patients who could be "trusted" to do the job properly. Joe "worked" periodically out of this office.

Throughout his stay at the hospital, Joe was assigned to a variety of "jobs." These were unpaid positions, and if not done willingly, even enthusiastically, were seen as a proof of mental problems.

Polishing Blocks

In old photos of the State Hospital, one sees an interesting contrast; walls and furniture may be shabby, patient grooming may be minimal, the food may look bland, BUT the floors absolutely gleam. The source of these shining tile floors was a therapy in which patients pushed large blocks of wood covered with cloth back and forth down the floors. These polishing blocks came in four sizes, weighing as much as sixty pounds. A broom handle fit into the block to push it, but, for sake of safety, the handle was not permanently attached and therefore could not be used as a giant hammer-type weapon.

Patients were assigned this task on a Monday-Wednesday-Friday schedule for two hours, 3:00–5:00 p.m. The less the staff liked you, the more paraffin wax was shaved off a block onto the floor. Water was then added and that made the task even more difficult. As someone who frequently spoke his mind, Joe was assigned to this task with a lot of wax and a lot of water. This chore was often a punishment for minor infractions of the rules. The stated therapeutic goal was as an opportunity to work off stress through physical labor and to train patients for meaningful work. Of course, there never have been a lot of block-pushing jobs. . . .

Tunnels

All buildings at the State Hospital were connected by underground tunnels. These allowed for the transportation of food, laundry, and supplies. Patients and staff could use these tunnels to move from building to building during inclement weather. It was also a more secure method of moving patients who were an escape risk. Long-time patients knew the tunnels so well that even in a power outage, they could navigate their way safely. The tunnel entrance by the Rh building had a large set of fans and an area behind the fans where patients could go for a "quickie." Sex between patients was forbidden by state law and hospital rules, so any intimacies had to be obtained in out-of-the-way places. That is, if one's interest wasn't crushed by the tunnel mice, bugs, and daddy long legs, not to mention the psychotropic medications. Sex usually involved three people; two to participate and a third to serve as look-out.

Joe is convinced that some type of libido-suppressing chemical was added to the patients' food, an "observation" made by a large number of former patients.

State Hospital Friends

The fellow patients Joe admired were those independent spirits like him, individuals who would not "suck up" to the staff. One friend was called "Tarzan" and was a tall, big man who followed the rules but was his own person. Another friend was "Che Che," who, except for stature, was like Joe, and was no fool. Joe remembers one patient who was supposedly his cousin. Jay D. Jay was a "yes-man and follower, a brown-noser who stayed in good with the staff." On one occasion, Jay turned in Joe and his friends for smoking in an unauthorized area. The transgressors got time in the quiet room; Jay D. was rewarded with a transfer to an open ward.

Activities and Pastimes

Joe wrote for the hospital patient newspaper, *The Spotlight*. While some copies are included in the Lincoln Regional Center museum, none with Joe listed as an author could be located. Joe also learned all the standard recreational activities on the ward: chess, monopoly, rummy, canasta, spades, hearts, Chinese checkers, poker and, ironically, The Game of Life.

Dances were held at the Auditorium building on a monthly basis. This was not an easy task for people taking Thorazine and other psychotropic medication. Medications were given at 4:00 p.m., and by the time the dance started at 7:00 p.m., most of the patients were not feeling much of anything. These drugs interfered with the body's sense of rhythm and movement; the most common dance was not the waltz or two-step, it was the "Thorazine Shuffle." Male patients danced with female staff members, female patients with male staff. Attendance was compulsory for all staff and patients. Ward staff and nurses wore their "whites" and caps, and patients wore their "best." Patients who could not stand or walk attended in wheelchairs, and staff would twill them out onto the dance floor. Of course, no "close dancing" was allowed; a stick over twelve inches in length was used to judge if someone was dancing closer than was "safe."

Cigarettes

Joe developed his smoking habit at the State Hospital when he was in the Security (now Forensics) Building. He says he started for "self preservation." Each patient was assigned a chair in the day hall and smoking was allowed with clip-on ashtrays at each chair. With everyone around him always smoking, he decided to join in, since he was already inhaling so much second-hand smoke.

Smoking and mental hospitals have a long, joint history for patients. In part, it is an issue of boredom. In 2000, the Harvard Medical School completed a study that indicated that fifty percent of the cigarettes in this country were consumed by people with a mental illness diagnosis. In part, this is because cigarettes appear to help lessen the side effects of some of the psychotropic medications like Thorazine, one of the drugs Joe was given. And nicotine, being the addictive drug it is, does not let go of its victim just because he is no longer taking medications.

Psychotropic Medication

Joe describes the medication he took as feeling like you were "looking through gauze." Thorazine, an antipsychotic medication, first began being used at the State Hospital in the late 1950s. It was seen as a miracle drug that would revolutionize psychiatric care. Thorazine and drugs that followed are credited for the release of thousands of patients from the State Hospital.

Most patients during the time of Joe's stay were on one or more psychotropic drugs, as was Joe. As needed, doses of the same drug were available for the patient if someone became especially agitated, angry, or psychotic. These medications were available in tablet, liquid, and injectable forms; if a patient was suspected of spitting out their pills, a liquid dose or "shot" was given. The early antipsychotic medications did help to control hallucinations and delusion, but came with a long list of side effects that included dry mouth, sensitivity to sunburn, drowsiness, low blood pressure, difficulty with movement, and even tardive dyskinesia, an irreversible brain disorder.

While these medications, and their more effective and less harsh prodigies, were instrumental in the release of thousands from institutions, it is important to note that in the years since his discharge from the State Hospital, Joe has never needed to use any of this family of medications and has not been hospitalized or under the care of any doctor for mental-health concerns.

LSD Experiments

Nursing notes on Joe from the State Hospital indicated that on August 18, 1961, two cc's of LSD (Lysergic Acid Diethylamide, a hallucinogenic compound) were given to Joe in an intravenous injection at 8:45 a.m. His blood pressure was monitored until 9:25 a.m. and he was returned to the ward at 9:35 a.m. Joe was eighteen-years-old at the time.

According to Dr. Klaus Hartmann, acting center superintendent, as reported by the Grand Island newspaper on 11-11-1979, as many as fifty patients at the then Lincoln State Hospital were given LSD by the late Dr. George Kleinschmidt. LSD was a widely accepted experimental drug at the time and, according to Hartmann, was given to patients before interviews with doctors as a treatment technique.

"The objective of the injection was to have the subject externalize various artistic and aesthetic experiences to provide the clinician with additional insight into the functioning of the subject," wrote Hartmann.

The drug was thought to have been especially useful for individuals with a diagnosis of sociopath or withdrawn schizophrenia. Others thought it was a way to test if a patient was truly psychotic or just "faking" their illness. If truly psychotic, the LSD would "blow the lid off" him.

In a twelve-page letter in response to twenty-eight questions later posed by Nebraska State Senator John DeCamp, Dr. Hartmann stated that, while there may have been payments to Dr. Kleinschmidt from the Sandoz drug company, no proof existed. Dr. Kleinschmidt was characterized as a "brilliant individual" with "phenomenal memory" but not good at keeping records.

Joe recalls at least three doses of LSD and would not agree with any of the above theories. He believes he was a "guinea pig" for the hospital.

Shock Treatments

Electroconvulsive therapy (E.C.T.) is still used in modern psychiatry, but its use is limited to major depression that does not respond to anti-depressant medications. During Joe's stay at the State Hospital, E.C.T. (or shock treatments) was a common treatment for a variety of diagnoses. Joe believes his treatments were motivated by his obstinate personality and as punishment. Joe's first tip-off of an impending treatment was a small blue pill in the evening. If he didn't get to go for breakfast, he knew for certain he was slated for a treatment. Those patients getting treatments laid down on treatment beds with sheet restraints and a pillow under their back. Four aides would then hold down each patient as the doctor worked his way down the row with the "shock box." A tongue blade wrapped in tape was placed between the patient's teeth. Conductive jelly was placed on each temple in preparation for the electrodes. No medications for anesthesia or muscle relaxation were given, so the patient would have a "grand mal" seizure. Usually treatments were given three times a week for seven weeks. Joe received 158 treatments in total. Joe experienced the most common side effect, memory loss.

Sterilization

Joe was sterilized soon after his sixteenth birthday. He reported to the medical unit of the State Hospital where he was asked to lie on his back on a treatment bed. A drape was hung so he could not see himself from the waist down. He was given a comic book to read while the procedure was completed. He remembers that they did not let him finish reading it before he was sent back to the ward.

Sterilization of those with "mental illness" was a result of the American Eugenics movement, which gained force at the beginning of the twentieth century. It was an extension of Darwin's theories of natural selection and the movement's goal was to ascertain that only people of superior intelligence and character would perpetuate the human race. This same movement backed the research of German eugenicists. One organization of the early

1900s was the American Breeder's Association (ABA), whose goal was to "emphasize the value of superior blood and the menace to society of inferior blood." In 1924, they began their successful state-by-state drive to adopt compulsory sterilization laws. In 1936, the superintendent of the Alabama Insane Hospitals told other physicians in the system that compulsory sterilization must be used broadly enough or "euthanasia may become a necessity."

Ironically, during World War II, the shortage of doctors caused the number of sterilizations in institutions to drop greatly. Eventually, scientific research refuted the genetic basis of much of the eugenic assumptions. State laws were changed to acknowledge the right of patients in the state mental health and mental retardation institutions to not be subjected to sterilization. These changes came too late for Joe, whose life and future were irrevocably changed that day at the State Hospital.

Even if Joe had given "voluntary" written consent for E.C.T. or sterilization, the inherently coercive atmosphere of the institution precludes it being legally valid.

Restraints and Seclusion

Joe remembers both the use of restraints and seclusion for himself and others. Restraint belts were made of leather and were applied to the waist, legs and arms. These belts were then attached by leather straps to the bed frame. This arrangement of five points of restraint was sufficient to render the patient immobile. The stated purpose of using "leathers" was to protect the patient from harming self or others. In Joe's case, he believes they were used more as a punishment, and far too often and too long. Only staff had the key device to remove the restraints. Seclusion rooms were simply small rooms with no furniture or bathroom facilities. The "padded cell" of movie fame never existed at the State Hospital. The window in the quiet room was covered with a screen. The door had an observation window so staff could check the patient. A bucket was provided for #1 (urination); for #2 (a bowel movement), one had to hope you were allowed to use the bathroom down the hall. Joe also remembers cameras in the room to monitor his behavior, sleeping on the floor of the quiet room with only a towel for a blanket, and being shackled by a chain to the wall. Liberal doses of medication were combined with seclusion and restraint so one's ability to resist was greatly decreased.

Institutionalization

"Borderline Mental Retarded." This is the only diagnosis Joe was aware of ever being awarded. This label was given to him by a judge in Omaha whom he had never met. Joe recalls no testing, no interviews. He was also treated for a seizure disorder but he denies ever having a convulsion. Joe recalls being given Thorazine 150 mg. four times daily. This is a phenothaizine drug, one of the first ever used at the State Hospital. It is an antipsychotic medication used to treat thought disorders that include hallucinations and delusions. Joe states he never experienced those symptoms.

The process of becoming institutionalized is an insidious one. As more and more daily responsibilities are assumed by the institution, the individual develops growing dependence on the structure of the hospital. When you get up, go to bed, what you eat, what you watch on TV — all are controlled by others. Patients and staff alike are not immune to these effects. Decisions are made based on orderly operations of the institution and what will work best for the greatest numbers. Baths are not when one needs or wants one, but on schedule "for everyone's convenience."

To be raised in an institution is, to the very core, a study in ambivalence. Joe lacked the role model of parents who progressively push the baby bird out of the nest while demonstrating what it means to be a grown-up. Even when parents are not the best of models, their efforts may have a less deleterious effect than an institution. For any person raised in such a setting, both love and hate function simultaneously. In Ken Kesey's *One Flew over the Cuckoo's Nest*, Randall P. McMurphy is shocked to learn that, unlike him, most of the patients are there voluntarily. All day they complain about the staff, the food, and the lack of services. But, they have also become dependent on the hospital and those very staff members. Walking away from all that control/protection becomes a very scary proposition. And the hospital, by its very nature, creates the dependency it then denounces in the patient as "laziness" or "hospitalitis."

There is a tendency to ask Joe, "Who were the good staff, the ones who were nice to you? And who were the bad staff, the abusive staff?" The problem with this dichotomy is that both those who are kind and those who are not rob the patient of his independence. Institutionalization occurs because kind people *and* not-so-kind people think they know what is best for the patient. Their position of power allows staff to control the life of the patient. There are times when a person needs to be cared for by society, when that individual is a danger to themselves or to others. In Joe's case, that was never a question; he is consistently referred to as not a dangerous person.

Joe's State Hospital Records

On March 19, 1957, Dr. E. C. dictated the following admission note: "This patient was admitted to the hospital on March 15, 1957, having been transferred from the Boys' Training School, Kearney, Nebraska by authority of the Board of Control, for observation and treatment of a mental disorder. He is 14 years of age, single, Catholic, and his education is unknown. His father, Joseph Soukup, Sr., lives at 502 So. 20th St., Omaha, Nebraska *(Joe's father died on August 20, 1956, and already had been dead for six months when this staffing was held)*. The patient was admitted to the Boys' Training School, Kearney, Nebraska on December 31, 1953. He has also been in Father Flanagan's Boys' Home, Boys' Town, Nebraska."

A clinical history completed by a Mr. M. repeats verbatim the social history done at Kearney.

On February 6, 1958, a Social Service Report was dictated by a DLK, stating, "Joe has been doing about the same on the ward. However, he had been around when the worker talked with other children and wanted the same opportunity. He chatted some about his relatives and the fact that he has not been visited for a time. He would like to also see his sister in Omaha and wondered if the worker could take him there when he goes to Omaha. He was informed this could not be done, but Joe could continue writing to her and perhaps some day they would be able to visit each other again. *(Joe believed he was in a type of orphanage; he had no idea what a "State Hospital" was. He tried to use the coping skills he had to establish rapport with the staff. He was hungry for attention, a very normal need.)*

"Joe gets restless easily and after talking for around ten minutes he wanted to return to the ward. The worker carried the conversation on for a short time and then decided to take him back. Joe is still, in the worker's opinion, nearly the same as before. Any improvement will probably take a long time. Joe will be seen when he asks for an interview because he does not do this very often."

On June 25, 1958, DLK entered, "Summary of observations and contacts: Joe must have spent the better part of his life learning how to get along. He certainly has displayed the charactistics [sic] of a kid who wants to be liked. In fact, Joe's natural (or unnatural) unselfishness has been his trademark on the ward. However, if he has been pushed too hard, Joe has rebelled to some extent and has stood up for himself with the other patients. During the last part of April and almost through May, he seemed to have a delusion about leaving. The ward notes were almost the same from day to day in that they mentioned Joe was packing his suitcase or making final arrangements to leave the hospital. It is hard to determine why he was doing this. Speculation was that he was bidding for attention or testing the personnel. It began to appear that Jo's [sic] fantasies were actually delusions. During the last part of May the truth came out, and Joe specifically told the worker on June 9 why he had been 'pulling our leg.' *(This entire episode seems painfully obvious: Joe wanted to go 'home.')*

"Joe's sister has been living in the St. James' Orphanage. Joe and she have been close in their life. The only communication they have had for the last several years has been correspondence. Joe has been fairly well satisfied with this arrangement; however, during the last month he has not been hearing from her. This caused him a lot of anxiety and he wanted out so badly that he began to make up stories about it. He claims that he was fully aware that plans were not developing for him. Now that he knows that his sister has been adopted and will not be writing him, Joe has settled down or at least is not claiming that he is leaving every day. The news that they would be separated permanently hit Joe pretty hard. It was explained that he could try and locate her after they were grown and that nobody could keep them apart after that. This was some consolation for Joe but evidently not enough. *(This forced separation without even the ability to write seems very unfair to both Joe and Pat, as it would to almost anyone.)*

"Mr. E. was conferred with on May 28 after he had told Joe that his sister was being adopted. He stated that Catholic Charities was [sic] still interested in the boy and they wondered how long it would be before he could leave. Mr. E. felt that from the interview it might be a long time yet and wanted this confirmed. As Joe has not been brought up at Staff or discussed in conference for some time, it was not possible to tell Mr. E. how long it would be. *(This would appear to be a clear admission of ineptitude on the part of the staff. Clearly there was no treatment plan or anticipated date of discharge. Nor was there any evidence of criteria for discharge beyond the vague following statement.)* However, the worker opinioned [sic] that the patient might be around for quite a few months yet. In order to help Joe through his period of depression the worker wrote to Catholic Charities and asked about Joe's other relatives. Mr. E. wrote back and gave a list of relatives living in Nebraska who Joe might contact. This list will be given to the boy in the near future.

"Joe has been seen occasionally and worker is going to try to get around to him more often as Joe responds so well. The ward notes during the last part of June suggest that Joe is becoming more open in ways. He refused to do ward work on one occasion but finally consented. Another reference notes that Joe had an argument with another patient who is prone to be withdrawn. Perhaps until this boy works through feelings about the loss of his sister he will appear to be more disturbed." *(A 'Catch-22' situation. If Joe doesn't show emotions it's a problem; if he does, it's a sign of mental illness and affirms his being in the right place.)*

On November 18, 1958, a staffing was held to review Joe. Seven doctors, seven social workers, three activities department staff, one vocational rehabilitation worker and several members of the nursing staff first met with Joe, then reviewed his case." *(Staffings in which a patient enters the room and sits before over twenty staff were an accepted medical practice and may still be in some areas. Joe was fourteen-years-old at the time of this meeting. The pressure must have been tremendous. How anyone can see this as a fair method of diagnosing or treating a patient is beyond common sense. Joe remembers this staffing. Three doctors asked questions and the rest of the group "just gawked.")*

Dr. R. G. dictated the following note that included a history of Joe's placements to date and then stated, "According to his home and background, his mother is dead and his father is living in Omaha. *(Apparently the staff still had not heard about Joe Sr.'s death. More likely, they were simply reading from previous records. This practice allows one-time errors to become long-term history.)* They were both alcoholics, mistreated the children, kicked them around the house and made them look after themselves *(there is no proof that any of this was true of Joe's father).* In the various schools which he has been in, there was some activity between him and some other boys sexually. He cannot make close relationships with people and seems to have a vivid imagination. He has been very untruthful at times and he seems eager for attention and affection. He was examined psychologically by Mr. S. and he has a full IQ of 78, but it is felt that he perhaps may be higher than this in regard to other abilities. Evidently his home situation was in such a mess that he was taken from the home and placed in various institutions for a long time. At staff today he seemed quite willing to come in and talk to us, he didn't seem to be too uncomfortable, although a little anxious. He said he has been in the hospital for approximately six months, was brought from Boys Town to the hospital and then from Kearney, etc. He said that he feels like people like him, but at first he doesn't trust people, he has to get to know them, like them *(Being cautious about who one gets close to would seem a sign of mental health; State Hospital staff, probably because they felt they were good, helpful people, had the expectation that patients would immediately trust and confide in them. To not do so was a sign of a problem.)* and he also has a tendency to tell false tales. It has been observed that he likes to get close to people or at least try to get close to them and tries to say the right thing to get attention or affection. In group therapy he is pretty bold and pretty blunt in some of his statements to the other children. It is difficult to know what to actually prescribe for this youngster. He is tall for his age; in fact he wears a size fifteen shoe [sic]. He doesn't know how to get along in society and he hasn't been able to adjust to it. Perhaps as he gets a little older, he will learn more and more how to take care of himself and live with people.

Diagnosis: Adjustment reaction of adolescence. (54.4) (The American Psychiatric Association code.)

Prognosis: Fair to guarded. Perhaps he may lose some of his tendencies as he grows older to mingle more with people and have more object relations and spend less time in fantasy formations. It was felt that he was not psychotic at this time.

Recommendation for Treatment: He should probably return to Kearney where he can enter in a full scale school program. Perhaps when he is old enough and eligible for it, he can have Vocational Rehabilitation and all the help that he needs and that is required to make the satisfactory citizen."

On January 29, 1959, DLK summarized interviews from January 13 to January 29: "Joe (now age sixteen) was given an opportunity for regular interviews during the first part of January. He responded eagerly, fearfully but punctually. It is impossible for him to express any strong negative feelings and humor was used during the last two interviews to help him feel more at ease. Then Joe got to laughing about something that was said and continued for five or ten minutes. This is not hysterical but showed a great deal of underlying tension. The area being talked about was his passivity and how he has 'doled out' his possessions to other people in effort to win their affection. When the conversation lagged, Joe picked it up hurriedly as if silence would break the tie between him and the worker. The patient constantly sought reassurance that he was not being too forward or discussing irrelevant material. His hyperactivity was contagious and it is hard for the worker to keep from being carried away at times.

"Joe was transferred to a new caseworker, Mr. G., during the first part of February. This was done because the patient is now in adult service. Also, Mr. G. will be able to give more time to him."

A note by RG (presumably Mr. G.) was entered on February 11, 1959: "A telephone call was made to the C-Center requesting an interview with Joe Soukup at the office of the social service. In a very short time Joe was in the office for interview. He was breathing so hard and could hardly speak. Worker asked Joe if he came running from his ward, he said 'yes.' Joe was encouraged to keep still until he is rested up and then we could go ahead with the interview, but he seemed so anxious to talk to the worker and asked worker to keep on talking. Evidently this young man is hungry for human relationship and for that reason he was running to see the worker. Worker introduced himself to him as his new social worker. Joe accepted this very readily especially since worker had few brief contacts with him previously.

"The ward attendant gave worker the impression that Joe has been in difficulty lately and did not explain the exact problem. When worker asked Joe what are the difficulties he has had on the ward lately, he explained that while he was working at the Greenhouse, he was accused of stealing a watch which was found under his pillow. He stated that he has never seen this watch and knew nothing about it. Patient thought that, maybe, one of the patients put it under his pillow. Joe, according to his own report, had no difficulty in stealing in the past and this was the first time he was accused of such behavior. This activity was checked with other personnel who know Joe and they felt that he was not involved in similar behavior in the past.

"Joe gives the impression of a nice, friendly, young man, who is cooperative in doing anything to please interviewer and this may be to him the only way of gaining acceptance and approval. When we discussed school situation with him he believes that his grades have always been A's and B's with the exception of one or two C's throughout his education. He finished the ninth grade and is anxious to further his education. This will be explored with him in later date."

On February 19, 1959, RRG wrote, "Joe came an hour before the time appointed for interview. This may indicate some of his anxiousness and desire to talk to someone who would listen to him. Since there was no office available at that time, the interview was conducted in the hall. Throughout interview it was difficult to keep his attention. He seemed easily attracted by others in the hall, especially if someone were passing by. Joe related quite easily with the worker and seemed to cooperate considerably throughout the interview. He talked about his desire to be a physician. That seemed to be one of his fantasies. It was necessary to talk with Joe that this was too high of a goal for him, especially since he only finished the eighth grade. The worker had to explain to him what it takes in the length of time, education, and finances to reach the goal so Joe immediately dropped the desire to be a doctor. He substituted it for working in a grocery store carrying baskets of food to the car for customers. He believed that this may not require any further schooling, and he can do that any time he is released from the hospital. That revealed some of the instability of this young man and his poor judgment as changing from doctor to grocery boy. Joe asked the worker about the kind of work he can perform. It was really difficult to advise the patient what he can do or should do and assure him that through vocational rehabilitation he may be able to determine what would be the best for him. Our plan with the Vocational Rehability [sic] Department was discussed with him, and he seemed to be agreeable with any plans and decisions the hospital may make in his behalf. *(Staff seldom see the possibility of patients holding professional positions, and in truth, it rarely happens. There are cases of patients, even with a diagnosis of schizophrenia, who have gone on to graduate level work and taken positions in the very units in which they received treatment. Joe probably was unrealistic about occupations, but how would he know much about the world of work other than the occupations he observed around him. In the State Hospital system, the ones with the most power are the doctors; not an unusual fantasy for any sixteen-year-old.)*

"Joe brought out again his inability to trust anyone and put it this way: 'Since my parents did not trust me, how can I trust anybody in the world?' He believes that when people begin to trust him, he immediately kicks out and begins to distrust. That my [sic] be an indication to the worker that he does not want to be trusted.

"Joe believes that his father died in 1952 and that he saw him in the mortuary in Omaha and all the relatives were around. Although our records indicate that his father was still living at that time, Joe believes that they are feeding us with lies. He believes that his mother died one month before his father's death. He described the cause of his mother's death as cancer, and his father's, a heart attack. When Joe saw that the worker is not convinced, he changed the date. He said, No, his father died in 1955 and hasn't heard from him since then. This may be however, a death wish on Joe's part, as his father does not care for Joe. *(Joe's father died on April 17, 1953. The State Hospital has still not gotten this fact accurate. Even worse, the staff are using their error to label Joe as delusional!)*

"Joe has a hard time collecting his thoughts and organizing any discussion that may require thinking. Even in writing he admits that he does 'very poorly.'"

On February 25, 1959, RRG writes, "Joe came on time for the appointment. He seems to continue progressing, although slowly, in grasping reality situations. For example, the dream and goals which he has had to be a doctor suddenly dropped this time, and he feels that he is not capable of reaching such a high goal and intends to work on a farm, which may be realistic. He also gave the impression that he is able now to make more friends and related that to tell [sic] the people the truth rather than giving them an exaggerated picture. Joe's fantasies, as he sees them, have given the people a negative impression about him and now he feels that there is no reason to fantasy [sic]. Joe, however, needs considerable help to pull out from a life of fantasy and exaggeration.

"Joe again suddenly told about his father as a dead person. He told the worker that his father hasn't seen him for quite some time. This may be a part of his fantasy, yet Joe does not see his father as a living person as long as his father has no contact with Joe and does not give him an allowance. He needs to be encouraged to talk about his feeling toward his sister, and the separation experience which he has gone through."

An April 29, 1959, a progress note describes Joe as a ". . . large, over-grown person" who is "pretty well behaved." Concerns about work ethic and truthfulness were common themes Dr. J. discussed. On May 15, 1959, Dr. C. transferred Joe to R-00. A June 2, 1959, note by Dr. K. accuses Joe of stealing $40 from a Mrs. T. in her office on May 13, 1959. The note states, "Two days later he confessed that he took money and he did it because he wanted to make trouble in the hospital so that he will not be sent back to Boys' Town in Kearney." Boys Town is, of course, in Omaha, not Kearney. It is unclear how this action would have prevented a transfer since both Kearney (Reformatory) and Omaha (Boys Town) would be exactly where someone is sent for theft. On July 6, 1959, Joe was transferred back to L-2 for stealing and because he "threatened the ward attendants." No details of these threats are discussed and it is not known if the supposed threats were verbal or physical in nature. This report is inconsistent with all other records for Joe.

RRG entered a long note on Joe on December 2, 1959, stating, "Weekly interviews have been conducted with Joe on a supportive basis. Joe, at times, responded to these interviews and fairly well accepted a social worker relationship. At times, however, he flared up and was highly emotional in the interviews and cut them short. Sometimes he gets restless and moody and after five or ten minutes of interview he loses interest and asks to be dismissed and at times he does not even ask for a dismissal. *(The staff member assumes they alone have the right to terminate an interview; RRG may or may not have been aware of the inequality of power this statement revealed.)* Joe's behavior is very unpredictable and his personality can be described as immature." RRG goes on to describe at length a tutor who worked with Joe on English, math, and history. Like many plans, Joe was enthusiastic initially but lost interest over time. He then states, "After Joe was involved in several difficulties on the ward, he was deprived of his privileges, including this tutor."

RRG discusses the following in the same note, "Several visits were made with the social worker of the Catholic Charities in Omaha regarding Joe and his sister, Patricia. Pat was placed twice for adoption and in both cases it was an unsuccessful adoption so she had to be taken to St. James Orphanage. Presently, however, she is placed in a foster home at 846 South 36th Street, Omaha. Some of her letters to Joe were referred to the social worker. The letter gave the impression of her being a more mature and realistic girl. She was very supportive in all of her letters to Joe. This seems to please Joe and he identifies with her very closely. *(Note that no mention of Joe's father is included. One would assume the topic of Joe's father not visiting him, Joe's belief that his father was dead, etc., might have come up in the conversation. However, no correction is made in the record.)*

"Joe was seen on the ward today and he was highly upset because he was told that he would be allowed to have a certain amount of money on his account at the hospital and the balance would be referred to the county for his keep. Joe handed over to the worker sheets of writing of his expense since he was at the hospital and the amount he should have been having on his account at Bookkeeping. Joe was far from being realistic in his figure and seemed to have a certain degree of fantasy. He used verbal threats as to contacting his attorney about the decision of taking some of his money away and he also believed that he put the whole State of Nebraska in trouble. It was very difficult under these circumstances, to give support to Joe and the worker gave Joe the opportunity to talk out his fear, hostility and anxiety and gave very little response. Joe, in worker's opinion requires a great deal of attention although a close relationship is very threatening to him. Joe needs assurance and self-confidence so he tries to buy a relationship on the ward." *(Is it possible that Joe is angry that his money is being used to keep him in a place he doesn't want to be? Should someone who is not in an institution on a voluntary basis be required to use personal funds toward the cost of the hospitalization?)*

On December 30, 1959, Dr. A. noted that Joe was ". . . unusually tall and thin. Attendant reports that he eats abnormally large amounts of food but does not gain weight. He has no physical complaints nor symptoms. . . . On the basis of possible diabetes mellitus, we checked his urine this A.M. for glucose and found it to be negative. His FBS *(fasting blood sugar level)* was 116% mg. Thus diabetes is ruled out. We attempted a BMR *(basal metabolic rate)* test but could not gain the patient's cooperation in that he seemed to become salivated when the oxygen was started. Swallowing saliva at very frequent intervals badly interrupted the graph to an extent that it was wholly uninterruptible. When available, we shall administer a single dose of Povan on a basis that this man has an 'Oxyuriasis' infestation *(pinworms).* Pharmacy assures me that they will have the above drug available shortly." A note on February 7, 1960, noted Joe had regained three pounds.

No further progress notes were on the same sheet of paper (doctor's notes) until an August 1, 1960, transfer note from L-1 to L-2.

On August 9, 1960, an ME *(social services worker)* stated, "The patient was seen several times in July by the worker. The patient *(Joe is now seventeen-years-old and still delusional about his father!)* continues to believe that both of his parents are dead and has a fantasy of having been institutionalized since he was four years old. On the basis of the patient's record, it does not seem that regular interviews would be fruitful. The patient requested the worker to obtain a wrist watch for him and the request has been passed on to Mr. L. (Rejected by Parole and Discharge August 10, 1960.)"

On September 7, 1960, ME notes a conversation with Joe in which he expresses a desire to cooperate with the hospital and requests that staff be tougher on him. Joe "wished the attendants would be like those in Kearney who did not ask, but told him to do contain [sic] chores and he then had no choice."

ME discusses Joe's money. "He also wondered why he was allowed to have $700 in his patients trust fund account while other patients were not allowed to have more than $300. He wished that his would be cut down to $300 because he doesn't want to be any different from other patients. Nothing will be done about his account at the present, but the worker suggested to Dr. K. that Joe probably should be considered for work downtown if he is willing to do so.

"Joe was interviewed September 7. He said he would be quite happy to work downtown if the doctors here, who 'have the controlling interest,' decide he should do so. He did not think that his own feelings about it had much to do with the decision but said he preferred the work downtown to being at the hospital and not doing anything. The Parole and Discharge Committee will be asked to consider a referral to the Vocational Rehabilitation Office for the patient."

Then on December 15, 1960, the next progress note states, "Joe is nearly eighteen years of age. He came to my office asking 'could I tell him why he is an inmate here?' I told him that as nearly as I could determine it 'it was epilepsy'. I have gradually made some changes in Joe's treatment and he has not had a major seizure for 90 days. Joe tells me that he and his sister own a lot of property in Omaha, David City (a farm there) and at Harvard (apartment house). An Omaha Atty. is guardian of Joe and his sister (his parents deceased when he was a small child). *(There is no accuracy in this statement. Joe's parents never owned any property.)* Joe has been denied LP *(Limited Parole – an interesting term usually associated with a correctional setting)* in the past for petty thieving. . . . but since having his LP 6 months age [sic], there has been no incidents of kleptomania. It is my feeling that intensive research by Social Service might permit this young man to have an ID and possible ultimate discharge. Aside from one incident of petty stealing in the past 1 ½ years, Joe's deportment, his willing cooperation on small work detail, and other admirable tendencies, would all seem to justify more than usual consideration toward rehabilitation. I shall appreciate an intensive study of the situation by Social Service (I suggest first a conference with his Atty. to confirm his financial status and other matters pertaining that are not included in his record here). It is my understanding that he is a pay patient at the Lincoln State Hospital."

An entry labeled "February 16 to April 6, 1961, Summary of Contacts," dictated by someone with the initials "RC" discusses interviews with Joe in which a possible discharge from the hospital is considered. RC notes, "He didn't know where to go nor does he know what to do if he is ever released from the hospital. He doesn't have any special job that he would like to do and mentioned that he would like to do what the doctors want him to do. He added he has been doing what other people want him to do all his life *(one could say that this is very insightful on Joe's part)*. He is fearful that he might get into trouble again." Joe was disappointed to find out that an uncle who farms near David Cib, Nebraska, could not take him into his home." Joe is quoted as saying that he doesn't like to go to any other relatives because "they are all alcoholic, like my mother was."

In this summary, Joe expresses his dislike for Mr. E. from the Omaha Catholic Charities because Joe felt Mr. E. likes his sister better. Joe is quoted as stating he would like to work as an attendant at the hospital, since he knows all the routines. During this time period Joe applied for a job at Gold's Department Store but was turned down.

A May 1, 1961, note dictated by a JAF described a call from a Mrs. B., hostess at the Java Room at the Lincoln Hotel. Joe was apparently employed there but had not come to work. The note states that Joe had quit the job because he had a seizure on the previous day while at work. He is quoted as saying he was not going back to work, "At least, not for now, as I am afraid when I get a seizure I might hurt someone. Also, I have to get close to those girls."

A June 5, 1961, note by RC describes a busing job Joe held for three days at the Lincoln Hotel. "He felt that the work was too hard for him and that he was doing the job of three people. Apparently Joe was threatened by the women working at the dining room as they made much fun about Joe's tallness. Joe later appeared quite anxious due to the fact that he was unable to keep his job and he wanted to have somebody 'adopt him' out of the hospital." *(The writer lists the privileges Joe would like – freedom to go downtown, spend his own money – and assumes these requests are a compensation for his failure to keep his job.)*

On June 5, 1961, RC continues discussion of Joe's weekly sessions with the worker to "help him to solve some of his feelings of insecurity, ambivalence and self-esteem. He responded fast through the relationship with the worker, but apparently had very low tolerance for frustration." The note outlines unsuccessful efforts to place Joe with family, in Omaha agencies, or in independent employment. Joe is still asking to be "adopted out to a family who can provide not only supervision but also affection which apparently was denied to him as a child." RC does not see this as a possibility and suggests a potential placement in a nursing home or another hospital.

On June 23, 1961, Dr A., "L" building medical doctor, entered the following progress note: "This patient *(Joe is now seventeen-years-old)* has proven himself to be wholly unreliable in the matter of his defeating every conceivable effort to create an adequate adjustment. Mr. F. *(the "L" building day charge aide)* and his Department have been more than considerate in their efforts to assist Joe in the matter of rehabilitation. He has been assigned to most every work detail on the station, and always HAS FAILED *(capital letters added by Dr. A.)* after a few days experience on each of the several jobs *(although the words 'work' and 'job' are use frequently in these documents, these were really unpaid activities that patients felt pressured to accept in an effort to show they were well and able to make a go of it on the 'outside.' Joe believed he would never leave the State Hospital and therefore did not care about these 'work' assignments).* Presently I have just been called by Recreation Therapy to say that he has *failed [italics in original]* to report on the job to which I assigned him (by his choice) a few days ago. The therapist states that he is chumming around the ground with two girls (patients). *(Joe states that this was not true; even if it were, it is not exactly unusual behavior for an eighteen-year-old!)* In conference with Joe this afternoon he admits homosexual indulgences since he was eight years old *(during residence at the Boys' Training School and at the Flanagan Home in Omaha. He denies any such activities since being at Lincoln State Hospital.).* He is a notorious liar and all his statements should be evaluated on knowledge of his faulty veracity. I fronted for Joe for a groundparole *[sic]* almost a year ago. He has not to my knowledge abused his ground privileges other than his failures to conform to assigned work details. Presently he alleges that there are in Lincoln State Hospital two male patients that know about his abnormal sexual proclivities and have disseminated the information generally. This may be a paranoid defense for his irresponsible conduct.

I am puzzled as to how best treat this fellow. I doubt that EST *(Electro Shock Therapy)* is the answer. Deleting his ground privileges will not in my opinion alter his behavior. He is a known epileptic but since being placed on Elipten therapy his seizures are at distinctly minimal intervals."

Comments: Dr. A. is obviously exasperated with Joe. Sexual behavior by patients was not condoned and Freud's theories in regard to sexuality and same-sex behaviors were en vogue at this time. Certainly the concept of "sexual orientation" was not even considered. Add to this what we now know about the prevalence of same-sex experiences in adolescence, in Joe's case, this really signifies nothing of any predictive interest. "I fronted for him" indicates a level of personal involvement in which the patient's behavior becomes a reflection of the staff member's ability. In a future note, when Dr. K. gives Dr. A. a "barb" about counter-transference, he is probably on target.

On June 26, 1961, a Progress Note by Dr. A. stated: "This patient came to my office this morning and asked 'What kind of lies is Mrs. R. in Recreation telling about me?' I informed him that Mrs. R. had called me late last week stating that he had not reported for duty on recreation and asking [sic] if I know about Joe's failure. This is again one of many cases where this young man has failed to accept and carry out assigned duties.

"After the 'outburst' against Mrs. R. this morning I proceeded to tell Joe of the many instances where he has fallen down and violated the confidences placed in him by Social Service and by me. At the conclusion of the enumeration of these FACTS Joe pulled out his parole card and asked if I wanted it. I did and sent him back to his ward and phoned the Charge viz [sic] (*probably meant to type 'aid,' a misspelling of 'aide'*) 'as of now Joe has no further ground privileges.' His parting shot was 'I will do anything to get out of this rotten hole.' I fully believe that his ultimate residence will of necessity have to be the reformatory (*this statement was made even though Joe was never charged with any crime*). However, I should like very much to have Dr. K. study this man and make such suggestions as may seem to be indicated."

Two days later, on June 28, 1961, Dr. A. writes Joe's transfer note: "Dr. K. after receiving a carbon copy of my progressnote [sic] this date, called and advised that this patient be transferred to S-5 (*the highest level of security ward and the site of frequent use of shock treatments*) subject to approval of Dr. G. I feel that this transfer if accomplished will offer to Joe the type of therapy and discipline (*the use of the word 'discipline' is indicative of the writer's attitude toward Joe*) that I am unable to render on L-2. Dr K. may succeed in psychiatric therapy; but with complete deference to Dr. K's abilities, I yet feel that this irresponsible young fellow will wind up in the Reformatory. I fear that I have been far too lenient with him in an effort at rehab."

Joe was transferred to Security Unit 5 and Dr. K. assumed responsibility for his care. His note on June 30, 1961, seems to return Dr A.'s "barb" about his abilities by labeling Dr. A.'s reaction to Joe as "negative counter-transference."

Comments: In Freud's theories of therapy, counter-transference occurs when the psychiatrist or therapist has an emotional reaction to a patient that is in response to the therapist's own psychological issues or in response to unresolved feeling of the therapist to his/her own family or significant others.

Dr K. wrote: "Please see the extensive recent progress note by Dr. A. to the extent there's a negative counter-transference. He's getting very exasperated lately because Joe keeps sloughing off his various assignments. Dr. A. has gone a long way in trying to work with Joe but he doesn't have any basic drive and has extreme hospitalities, and gives various flimsy excuses why he can't work. We went so far as to place him in a job in downtown Lincoln and he quit after a couple of days 'because of this seizure.' He came here from the Kearney Reformatory Industrial School at age fourteen in 1957. He's now about eighteen. The main reason he came here was because of behaviorism, stealing and lying, but in the interim he had apparently a long chronic catatonic schizophrenic reaction manifested by hallucinations and various bizarre and magical thinking *(Joe believes this was never the case; however, large doses of psychotropic medication may have given the appearance of catatonia)*. Recently, is *[sic]* about one year ago, and incidentally apparently he got much better from the kleptomaniac. He used to pick up everything, rather skillfully too, but he's been on a ground freedom for about a year. He has a history of homosexuality and still is latently so, not overt, has made a fairly good adjustment in the L building, just cannot stick to an assigned task. He is of below-average to dull-normal intelligence, but he's not really deteriorated. This is probably not too much below his maximum. Dr. A. is exaggerating and has become somewhat exasperated, naturally so, so has Social Service because attempts to push him ----he just doesn't push. It is hoped that a structured atmosphere in the Security Building will change him. He allegedly has a history of epilepsy for six years and takes one Eliptin, 250 mg. and one Dilantin a day. Frankly, I think this is hysteria. He is not overtly schizophrenic now. He appears to be more of a passive-aggressive character disorder, usually affable, smiling, likes to run errands but resorts to lies if he's pulled down on responsibility. Incidentally, I investigated this matter of epilepsy. I checked with several aides in the L building and no aides here have ever actually seen him have a seizure and he finally admitted that he made it up. I believe this. I feel rather strongly that he is not epileptic, and he was on a very close ---- He admits he likes it here. He is lazy, he tells lies not as planned malice so much as to keep out of work, to protect himself. His kleptomania tendencies are under somewhat control now. I feel that Joe can control his behavior. He is not motivated to leave or to be self-supporting. It would take a year here under structured situation to motivate him. Patient is not psychotic now. Whether or not he was ever really psychotic or this was hysterical acting out, I don't know, probably was a transient psychotic reaction. His plans basically are to stay here the rest of his life. He has a very deprived background. The only relative is a 16-year old sister in Good Shepard Home in Omaha and apparently she is there for behaviorism." *(Joe states his sister was never in any trouble with the law or the orphanage.)*

On October 25, 1961, a B.M.S. enters a note that states that Joe is to have an eye exam and be fitted for glasses if necessary by a Dr. J.

The next progress note from Dr. K. is entered on November 22, 1961, when he transfers Joe back to the L Building. This is despite his June 30, 1961, recommendation that Joe remain in the Security program for at least a year. Dr. K writes: "Transfer to L-2. This long-time institutional orphan likes it in the hospital and was sent to the Security Building and we tried to cure him of his laziness, and we have tried to structure him, and he's been fairly good. He is harmless (*one of several references to Joe's lack of danger to self or others*). He used to be stickyfingered around the ground [*sic*] and he used to tell lies. By the way we cured him of lying about his seizures because he doesn't have any seizures and he gets no treatment for them and he knows we know. He needs to be kept under close surveillance and put in a highly structured situation and not allowed to roam. He'll be given limited parole in the laundry and if he doesn't work, he stays on the ward. We would be delighted to get him a job downtown if we thought he could hold it, and if he goes like a ball of fire around here for six months, we'll consider it again because he's about reached maximum benefits from hospitalization. He's of average intelligence and I have seen him when he was overtly psychotic, but he's not now. He's more of a passive-aggressive personality."

On December 15, 1961, Dr. A. acknowledged Joe's November 16 transfer to L-2. He stated: "This young man who I believe to be about 18 years of age is rather unique in his stature. He is probably six feet seven and weighs about 185 lbs. Joe is a chronic manipulator and is very cunning and flitting from one job to another. So much so that we had to exaction [*sic*] dicipline [*sic*] and send him to security for several months where Dr. K apparently solved the problems existing with Joe by some good heart to heart talks (*this comment might seem supportive to the layperson but really is a criticism when used in a psychiatric setting; doctors simply do not have 'heart to heart' talks and return a person to normal function*), pointing up many of his weaknesses. (*Joe never recalls even having a single session with the doctor. His contact with him was limited to when the doctor visited the ward and then the only thing he ever said to Joe was 'Hello.'*) Joe by his own right although his financial affairs are administered by a guardian in Omaha apparently has considerable wealth in the form of real estate and intangibles. (*There is no truth in this statement at all; Joe had no money whatsoever left to him by his parents. We believe he had Joe confused with another patient.*) At least he is fully able to purchase at any time and all times all sorts of expensive gadgets such as high fi [*sic*] and tape recorders, radios, watches, etc. He is known to be and has been for many years a known kleptomaniac but during the past nine or ten months have been no incidents relative to thieving by him. Presently he is doing very well on a limited parole as an errand boy for the ward. I am, however, watching him closely to see that he does not violate in any sense of the word the meaning of a limited ground parole. If he does and he fully understands the consequences, he will be returned to security as a dicipinary [*sic*] measure."

On August 2, 1962, Joe was transferred to R-7 but no reason for the transfer is noted. The next entry on the page in a notation on April 10, 1963: "Transfer note — This patient who was transferred from R to L-3 yesterday for misconduct on R is being traded *(an interesting choice of words in a hospital supposedly committed to making decisions based on therapeutic criteria)* by authority of Dr *[sic]* C. for William *(full name given but not included here)* presently on Security."

A May 9, 1963, Transfer note by Dr. G. states: "This patient has been in Security building for sometime *[sic]* having been returned there after being having *[sic]* ground parole periods on the north side of the institution. He was working for the conductors and evidently he got into some trouble with the aides and patients in assisting his return to the Security situation. Since being back over there he got along well got into no particular trouble in his care as felt we should try him again in a more liberalized area of control, so as of May 9, 1963 he was transferred from the Security building to A-4. His ground parole was re-in-stated *[sic]* and he was assigned to work for conductors where he had been employed prior to his return to the Security unit."

But within two weeks, Joe was in trouble again. Dr. K writes on May 17, 1963: "This patient was returned while I was on leave to A-4 to work as a conductor, I have no objection; he has worked here before, he also has gotten fired. Joe is lazy, he has been known to tell lies, I don't think he is very dangerous or malicious, but he has worn out his welcome with Dr. A. He told a native foreigner who was working in the ward that he should take his camel and go back to Arabia and for this reason, he was sent to security. *(Not the most politically correct thing to say but hardly merits a transfer to the security unit!)* Joe is outspoken and he really doesn't have any reason to be. He is very institutionalized and he admits when he comes down to it. He will quit his job, fall back on some excuse, because he likes it in institutions and he is really fearful of getting out.

"Patient is overtly delusional, I see him as an inadequate character, incidentally, he has had fairly long standing at least borderline schizophrenic episodes *(perhaps the delusion about his dead father)*, but these are invariably mixture of malingering, and Joe can be likeable. I do not recommend any case work, as he gets a little frightened here, especially when somebody talks discharge *[sic]* just what we will do, I don't know but his case should come up with the possibility of job placement, Goodwill and that sort of thing. He was evaluated a few days ago by a psychiatrists and others from NPI, Dr. B. for the possibility of going there for rehabilitative placement. We hope they will take him, maybe the change of atmosphere will help *(when in doubt: transfer)*. He is harmless, but he will never make more than a marginal adjustment especially if the best deal is to try to find an institutional like placement for him."

On June 5, 1963, Joe was given a psychological evaluation by T. P., M.S. Assistant Psychologist which was co-signed by S. K., Ph.D. Chief

Psychologist. Joe was twenty-years-old at the time. The tests used for the evaluation were the WAIS, MMPI, Rorschach, Graham-Kendall, DAP. The report is as follows:

"Observations of behavior: The patient is an awkward, gangly boy who was overly polite initially, but as time went on his behavior became rather humorous and still later somewhat cynical and sarcastic. It is apparent from his behavior that he has been the object of ridicule and jokes by other boys and that he expects adults in general to disapprove of him and also make castigating remarks. Because of this expectation he seems to adjust his behavior to bring out rejection from other people. In spite of this humorous, sarcastic type of behavior the patient appeared to be extremely anxious and eager to succeed. Whenever he would fail he criticized his own performance and would wring his hands. He cooperated well on the tests and tried to do his best.

"Analysis of tests: Intellectually, the patient obtained an IQ of 82 which is in the Dull Normal range. His answers were impulsively given. It is felt that on the basis of his performance on other tests that intellectually he performs at least in the Average range and that anxiety significantly impaired his performance on the intellectual test. He showed signs of possible organicity on this visual motor performance and his understanding of interpersonal situations is grossly impaired. He does not know how to get along with people

"Emotionally, there are indications of a marginal adjustment concealed behind a façade of denial, cynicism and joviality. Clinically, the picture is that of an extremely defensive and guarded sociopathic character disorder. Underlying this façade however, are indications of anxiety, feelings of rejection, and need for support and approval, and a potential for some rather unusual thinking. He is not the typical sociopath because he shows a great deal of diffuse anxiety, feelings of inferiority, and a general dissatisfaction with himself. If one could penetrate the sociopathic shield with which this patient protects himself one would probably find a very scared, anxious boy who is unsure of this own abilities especially in terms of being accepted and interacting satisfactorily with others. The Rorschach indicates the potential for obstinate behavior, but also shows more psychotherapeutic potential than is evident at first glance. If a therapist could tolerate the antagonism which the patient would manifest in therapy it is quite possible that this boy could learn to make a better adjustment than he has. Since he expects to be rejected by other people and helps to create a situation so he will be rejected, it is doubtful that any outside placement would last very long before the patient would either quit or be fired. Intellectually, the patient could perform certain jobs on the outside as long as they did not involve close supervision or demand a great deal of social interaction."

No further progress notes are entered on Joe until almost a year later, on April 27, 1964, when Joe went downtown on a day pass and did not return for two days. Again on October 8, 1964, Joe walked off and did not return until November 10, 1964. An October 27, 1964, a note by A.L. stated the hospital had been contacted by Mr. E. of the Catholic Charities in Omaha informing them that Joe was staying with his sister Patricia. Mr. E. requested $60 per month from the hospital for Joe's living expenses. The plan was to place Joe on an indefinite parole and to have Patricia in charge of Joe's money. Dr. G. promised to consider the proposal.

On December 3, 1964, Dr. C. noted: "This patient is now 21 years of age. He came to this hospital for the first time on March 15, 1957. He has formerly been in Kearney, the Reformschool [sic]. He ran away from the hospital, R-00 on 10-8-1964, went to Omaha, and had trouble with his sister and his sister's boyfriend. Therefore he called Dr. C. and was returned to his hospital, L-3, on November 10, 1964. Patient has had about 25 grand mal treatments (electroconvulsive treatments) from 1958 to 1961. He has been on R-OO an open ward for one year. He tells many tales which are not always true."

On April 30, 1965, Dr. C. records a request from Joe to transfer to the Security building; his request was granted.

On August 15, 1965, Psychiatric Case-Aide B. N. made the following entry: "Joe seems to be adjusting probably the best of any person on S-1. He is not a runner for the Security Building. He has taken a number of trips downtown to go to the movie and buy records. He is very trusted on the ward; he does not say much but what he does say, usually makes half way good sense. The other patients like Joe very much. He is easy to get along with and for the most part, keeps his mouth shut. When Joe seems to go griping the loudest, it usually means that he wants what he is griping against the most. In other words, he is the sort of person who will save any used cake while he is fighting to get a piece of cake. If Joe is allowed to ventilate his feelings and one does not get too concerned over what he is saying, that is that he is making a real threat, Joe will never pose as a real problem for anybody. His abilities will always be limited but he should work out satisfactorily in another building if too much authority is not given to him."

An August 17, 1965, a note by Drs. K. and F. review Joe's participation in weekly group therapy sessions. Five security patients participated in the group. They stated, "Joe Soukup resists passively and explicitly, saying nothing unless asked, and pointing his resistance out." On August 27, 1965, Joe was transferred back to R-00.

On February 8, 1966, Joe again "escaped" from the State Hospital, returning on February 18, 1966. Joe stated he had been staying with his sister who asked him to return to the hospital.

Dr. P., on August 5, 1966, dictated a transfer note, moving Joe from R-00 to L-3. He stated, "Joe has been getting increasingly disturbed. Evidently he has not been getting along with other patients on the ward and he hasn't been getting along too well with the personnel in the Canteen. He requested and has requested several times a transfer to the L Building because he was afraid of what he might do and it is felt that he might either run away or cause some disturbance with other patients who have shown him quite a good deal of hostility."

On November 22, 1966, B. N. wrote, "On the above date the worker saw Joe for the first time at the ward physician's request on a bi-monthly basis. This patient has had a difficult time adjusting. He has held a number of jobs, not sticking to any for very long. However, since being on L-3 self-government ward Joe has seemed to make friends and adjust quite well. He was elected as ward governor and seems to be quite proud of this: he handles it as a big 'responsibility.' The worker spoke to Joe in terms of the future, asking him what he wanted to do with his life. The patient expressed surprise saying 'no one ever asked me what I wanted to do before.' Joe certainly has had numerous chances to outside adjustment and the worker felt this may have been a bid for sympathy. Joe said he would think about what he'd like to do between this interview and the next.

"Worker felt that Joe needs support, but is not as unstable as he has been in the past and that some future planning is possible for him."

The next note by B. N. is on January 30, 1967, for "December-January" Summary of contacts: "Joe is extremely unstable; when this worker first started working with him he expressed a desire for Vocational Rehabilitation training, the next time he had an appointment he was deter-mined to go out and find a job on 'his own.' He went downtown with two other patients and applied at the State Employment Office. Their office called us to find out if he had permission to find a job. Miss C. asked about the possibility of Manpower Training for Joe. His ward physician and this worker both had the opinion that Joe would not stick with it, but that he should have the chance to make it if he is able. There are two other patients who will be taking the Manpower Training Program at the same time. With this support, Joe may be able to stay with this. He will receive training in janitorial and waiter work as well as having an opportunity to finish his high school education. Time can only tell what will happen. Classes started today, January 30, 1967."

On April 3, 1967, Dr. L. signed a Clinical History note. The first part of the note is not included in the records. Dr. L. comments on Joe's recent attempts at job hunting and Manpower. He states, "It is rather notable that Joe has kept at it for eight weeks at one kind of activity like this, and he is spending his own money by and large to go to school at 630 No. 48th Street."

A physical inspection is also included by Dr. L. "Mr. Soukup is a 24 year old white male, 6'6" tall, weighing 202 pounds, a youth who has very angular features and is beginning to show some maturity. Integumentary - The patient has numerous dark brown maculopapular mole like lesions over the chest anteriorally and posteriorally. He has a small depressed in the skull over the left frontal area at the hair line on the left from a light fixture falling on him from the gym when he was in Boys' Town. It was knocked down by repeated basketball throwing at the fixture in a rancous [sic] kid play on the gym floor. Skeletal - The patient has a marked long bone over development, but no prognathism. He is somewhat round shouldered. The joint motion is good throughout. The fingers are extra long and slender. Respiratory - The chest is long, well developed, and muscular. The expansion is very good throughout. Percussion note is resonant throughout. Auscultation reveals normal clear vesicular breath sounds throughout. Cardiovascular - Pulse is 100 - 130. The patient is quite hyper-responsive emotionally. There is marked lability of the basal motor system. The pulse is of good quality. The heart sounds are of good quality. The systolic first sounds are louder than the diastolic at the tricuspid, bicuspid, and apical areas of the heart. No murmurs were heard. Gastro Intestinal - Oral hygiene is good. Teeth are in excellent repair. Appetite is good. He has good nutrition. Bowel works well. There are no masses, tenderness, or rigidity. Genito Urinary - Nocuria, 2 or 3 times a night. He has had trouble with enuresis, but he is much better since he has been on a preparation of Geroniazol, a combination of Nicotinci acid and very minor doses of Metrazol. The enuresis is much better now. There is no dyuria, no difficulty otherwise. Endocrine negative. Neuromuscular - The ear drum reflex to light is good. The pupils are equal, concentric and react to light and accommodation. The color is hazel. Muscle development is excellent. The wrist, patellar and plantar reflexes are good.

"Impression - Excellent physical status in a young adult male. This is to be noted that the temperature is 98.4; pulse, 64; respiration, 14; blood pressure, $^{120}/_{60}$.

"Medication - Patient receives Probanthine, 15 mgs. with Dartal, 5 mgs. At bed time. Mellaril, 100 mgs. Is given t.i.d. Pertofrane, 25 mgs. t.i.d., Ritalin, 10 mgs. b.i.d. He receives Geroniazol, 1 tablet t.i.d. for enuresis." (Besides the probanthine for his stomach and the geronizol for his urinary system, Joe was on Mellaril, an antipsychotic with a maximum daily adult dose of 200 mg. – Joe was on 300 mgs. per day; Pertofrane, an antidepressant with a maximum daily adult dose of 300 mgs. – Joe was on 75 mgs. each day; and Ritalin, a central nervous system stimulant used for depression and attention deficit hyperactivity with a maximum daily adult dose of 40–60 mgs. – Joe was on 20 mgs. per *day. Joe recalls being on psychiatric medications most of the years he spent at the State Hospital. He also received additional doses of medication if the staff felt it necessary. Joe says he never asked to be on any of these medications. He was always cooperative and took the medication orally because he knew the alternative would be a "shot." No medication was sent with him when he left the hospital; this would be unusual for someone who supposedly had psychotic symptoms.)*

A caseworker, S. R., entered a progress note on November 13, 1967, stating she had been seeing Joe weekly for the past two-and-one-half months at his request. She notes working with Joe on his attitude toward vocational training, stating, ". . . it is hard to decide whether he wants training because he feels he will gain acceptance from the worker or that he realizes its importance to himself." It is decided he will continue at Manpower with custodial courses. Ms. R. goes on to state, "As to whether Joe will follow through with his training when it draws near to a close and begins to threaten his security here at the hospital, is a question to be answered at a later date." *(Joe was a client of both Manpower and Goodwill. His duties consisted of janitorial work and the laundry and repair of donated clothing.)*

On November 21, 1967, Dr. L. enters a transfer note from Ward L-3 to C-3. "This patient was transferred . . . for administrative purposes and for advance in selfcare and to provide better concerted effort in better nursing, aide, and medical services."

A March 25, 1968, document reviews previous history and refers Joe for rehabilitation services.

On May 1, 1968, a new caseworker, L. S. makes the following progress note. She states Joe has now been seeing her weekly for several months. She writes, "He would often complain that they were fruitless (sessions) and demand more structure from the worker - often saying things like 'This is your meeting, ask questions'. Worker informed him that this was his meeting that if he did not wish to use it would be cancelled as there was no further point in continuing it.

"He expressed the feeling that he should be punished, that people know he did things wrong and that they were 'soft' on him. Apparently in order to do what he felt would 'please' the staff Joe brought in a newspaper article discussing an industrial plant which may open in about six months in Lincoln and might employ many people. Joe decided he wanted to work there and went to see Mr. Allen about it. Unexpectedly however he was at Goodwill within two weeks. This lasted only one week.

"On April 7 after he had been at Goodwill one week he visited with the worker. He expressed the feeling that people there were too 'soft' on him, that every time he did something wrong they gave him 'a giant lollypop [sic] and a pat on the back,' while he felt he should have been punished.

"He threatened to run away or 'take a vacation' and that this time be would go far and wouldn't be brought back easily. Worker asked him what he wanted her to do about it. He said she was supposed to notify someone in charge of his plans. Worker informed him she would not do this thereby in effect making his decision for him.

"On April 8 he left on the morning bus but did not report to Goodwill. At 10:45 that evening he reported to the police station requesting to return to the hospital. When he was returned to the hospital he demanded to be sent to Security Building, a request which all staff members ignored.

"He has informed the worker that he will no longer be in on Monday mornings. At the present time Joe is running errands, seems fairly cheerful and secure in his place in the hospital."

On May 17, 1968, Dr. P. entered the following clinical summary in a convalescent Leave Note, "Joe is going to live in a rooming house down town and he has a job that he had found by himself. The vocational rehabilitation people were not consulted about the type of job or the place that he intended to work and was quite proud that he had accomplished all on his own; however, Mr. A. of the Vocational Rehabilitation tells me that this man B. for whom Joe is going to work is not the most desirable sort of fellow to work for and does make it rather difficult for this type of worker to continue with the job. Joe tells me that in the four days that he had worked on the job he had been on three different shifts. This makes it rather difficult for anyone to adjust to outside living. It is indeed very difficult for a person that is used to the outside let alone someone like Joe that has lived here in an institution for the past 12 years; however, Joe is very enthusiastic and states that he thinks that he will be able to make a go of it and if he cannot establish a regular working pattern that he will continue to look for some other type of job at some other place where he can get a regular sort of working schedule fixed up. Joe is not on any medication at the present time and has been quite good for quite a long period of time. I asked the Vocational Rehabilitation people to have the men that worked down town check on Joe and the job occasionally and see that he does get along."

On June 17, 1968, L. S. entered another progress note. "Mr. Soukup was returned from Convalescent Leave June 17, 1968 by way of Douglas County Hospital. He has not yet said very much about the events which immediately preceded his return, and maintains that he does not know what happened to some of his belongings. He does say that he went to visit his sister in Omaha, and then went to Douglas County Hospital and asked to be admitted.

"Worker was called by the caretaker at his apartment who said that the mattress was ruined and the apartment needed cleaning and that the rent was up and a 30 day notice was required. Worker went to the apartment and gathered Joe's clothes and made arrangements with the caretaker for payment.

"It was found that a good many of Joe's things, such as clothes, record player and radio were missing. He has said that he sold the radio, but does not know that happened to the clothes. Apparently he bought an insurance policy from John Hancock and turned it in for cash value before he returned, as a check for $31.55 marked 'cash value' was in his mailbox at the apartment.

"The damages and rent at the apartment came to $70. This was paid to the First Realty Company and the money was taken out of Joe's account. Worker feels that Joe should pay this in a way that he will feel; therefore, his allowance is to be cut from 7 to 4 dollars per week until the $70 is paid up."

Dr. P. also dictated a "Return Convalescent Leave Note" on June 17, 1968. It noted his return from Douglas County also. He noted that Joe would be returning to his hospital job of "working" in the Dining Room in the R Building. He stated, "At the present time he (Joe) is quite hostile and not very cooperative but he was anxious to get back to his previous job."

On August 23, 1968, L. S. entered the following update, "Worker has been seeing Joe on a regular basis since his return from convalescent leave June 17, 1968. He was at first quite hostile and tried to place a 'blame' on the hospital for not preparing him better for living outside the hospital. He had, however, refused to accept any planning the hospital wanted to do with him, and even the services of Vocational Rehabilitation or any other services, and had instead insisted on moving outside the hospital, choosing his own living situation, and refusing any supervised setting. It was pointed out to him that he had to learn to accept responsibility for himself, and that when he got himself into something no one else was going to drag him out and apologize for him.

"Joe has been extremely resentful of the cutback in his weekly allowance which is to go on until the second week in November. This is to pay for the rent and damages done at the apartment which he had while he was on C.L. In the past two weeks or so he has been continually begging the worker to let him have more money from his account.

"On 8-18-68, he began working as a dishwasher at Diamond Jim's, a restaurant in the downtown area. He again requested money, but said he did not need it for car fare but because he wanted money to spend while he was downtown. This was denied as worker feels that he must feel both the responsibility of his 'debt' from C.L. and because it may very well be the lack of spending money which forced him to go out and get a job. He is to be paid on September 5 for the first time. He also requested money for uniforms both from this worker and another worker. A call to the manager where he works showed that uniforms are not needed for his job. He was quite angry about being denied the money.

"Joe definitely needs continued case-work service, and he will, furthermore, demand them. He has a great deal of ambivalence about the casework relationship and may appear an hour early for one appointment only to announce that he doesn't need to come any more, then appear at the worker's office demanding her time. It is questionable if he will ever leave the hospital, but if he does he will certainly need a very supportive environment. He sets himself up to be rejected and usually succeeds very well so that any job situation is usually very short lived."

On October 21, 1968, a new caseworker for Joe, L. D. enters the following note, "For the past several months Joe has been trying to manipulate the worker into getting him some extra money as his allowance was cut until the middle of November.

"On August 18, 1968, Joe found a job washing dishes at Diamond Jim's. . . . Joe did not remain at this job for more than a couple of weeks. It is not clear as to how or why he was terminated, though.

"On October 14, he went for a job interview at Milder Manor Nursing Home. He reported to the ward and worker that he had the job and had already worked four hours. He also requested $70 to buy uniforms and shoes. Worker checked with Mrs. B., the nurse in charge at Milder Manor, and she had not hired Joe and had no intentions of doing so at the present.

"It is felt that Joe should be restricted to the grounds until he can learn to handle himself. This will be discussed with the ward doctor and the aides."

On February 17, 1969, L. D. wrote the following, "Worker has been seeing Joseph Soukup on a regular basis for the past several months. He asked for these meetings with the purpose of finding a job downtown. However, worker has been refusing to give him permission to look for work and has referred him to vocational rehabilitation. They have been very firm with him and have laid down some rules especially in personal hygiene.

"Joe has continued to see worker weekly. He has been the 'runner' for the R building since November and feels that this is a great accomplishment. He has also been getting quite involved with the Hospital Highlights (newspaper) and the volunteer services. Presently he feels very contented and has no desire to find an outside job or be placed on Convalescent Leave.

"On several occasions Joe has asked worker about Convalescent Leave planning for him, but at these times his bed-wetting problem has always been brought up. He did discuss this problem at great lengths with worker, but offered no remedy or solution for it. He believes that if he knows why he wet the bed, that it could be controlled.

"Joe has expressed a desire to talk about his goals and will continue to see worker. The worker has also talked with Vocational Rehabilitation the they think that they may be able to work with him too."

On May 8, 1969, Joe was told to leave the State Hospital, to be off the ground or law enforcement would be called to arrest him for trespassing. This sudden change of heart was prompted by a legislative bill, introduced by State Senator Marvel. The purpose of this bill was to force the release of all those State Hospital patients who were being held but never committed to the institution. The Department of Public Institutions (DPI), that branch of state government that oversees the State Hospital, quickly moved to cut their ties to any of these folks. Joe left the State Hospital on May 8. He had one change of clothing and a small amount of cash.

Dr. W., Psychiatrist and Acting Clinical Director, wrote the following Clinical Summary on May 8, 1969: "Joseph Soukup has been a hospital patient since March 15, 1957 when he was received as a transfer from the Boys Training School. He escaped from the hospital on numerous occasions. Finally in 1968 he was placed on convalescent leave, however he returned approximately one month later and again plans were made for his eventual release. He had accumulated money in his patient's account which should enable him to live comfortably until he is able to obtain a full time job. Mr. Soukup did not wish any assistance in locating a job. He stated that he wanted to leave the hospital and that he was 'not coming back'. Since his adjustment has been borderline while in the hospital setting, it is assumed that his adjustment will be borderline in the community. Since Mr. Soukup is over 21 years of age and did not wish to sign in as a Voluntary patient, it is felt that we no longer have any legal hold on this patient. He is of course non-psychotic and should be considered competent. Discharge Diagnosis: 1) Borderline Mental Retardation and 2) Inadequate Personality."

Joe left the grounds and walked downtown to the Trailways Bus Station and caught the bus back to Omaha. There he went to the Flatiron Hotel and took a job washing dishes to cover his stay in the hotel. There was no documented discharge planning, no help with locating a place to stay or employment. Joe grew up in an institution that now firmly rejected him. He doesn't know how he survived those first months, but he "just did." After sixteen years of state institutions housing, feeding and directing his every moment, freedom may be sweet but not easy. And it is the nature of institutionalization for the individual to have ambivalent feelings.

On June 11, 1969, Dr. P. recorded this follow-up progress note: "I saw Joe in my office today, 6-10-69. He was neatly dressed. His hair was nicely combed but he was unshaven. He stated that he had been out for 32 days and that he was too much of a softie for the outside world. He had been discharged and given $294 when he left here. Joe stated that this was down to about $50 in the bank and that he had a check for $76 for Social Security now in the Business Office which Dr. Coats authorized he be given to him [sic]. He stated that he had a job he hoped to get at the

University for $1.55 an hour. This would be considerably less than the money he had spent the first month. He stated that he has not learned to care for his money and spends it all on various books and entertainment. He also stated that he had no bed wetting problems. He is living at the Sam Lawrence Hotel. We will have to check on this with them if he stays long enough to start investigation.

"He is to come back to see me in one week."

Joe's records contain an entry on July 18, 1969, by a B. S. MSW (Master of Social Work), "Joe was discharged from the hospital on 5-8-69 as it seemed he had been here illegally since he was age 21. He was eager to leave and would not sign a voluntary admission to remain. He planned to go to Omaha as this was considered his home and he would be near his sister.

"Inquires began coming in from the Social Security Office, Voc. Rehab., etc. Each time a different address was listed. First, the Sam Lawrence Hotel, then the Y.M.C.A. We even received a call from Mrs. R. at the police station. She informed us that Joe showed up there one evening asking for supper and a place to sleep. She wanted to know what we wanted done with him as they could not hold him. She was quite censorious and almost demanding of a plan for Joe. Worker suggested he apply for help at the Lancaster County Welfare Department or see someone at the Southeast Psychiatric Clinic or Mrs. H. regarding board and room.

"Mrs. H. finally called us from the Lancaster County office requesting that we send the DA-5 and Social Services Summary to Douglas County, which is being done."

Joe stayed in Omaha for several months and then returned to Lincoln with the goal of extracting justice from the State. His search began by seeking legal representation. He learned the Lincoln bus system well as he tried to interest six different attorneys in his case. All rejected the case; Joe lacked the cash to retain a lawyer. They all told him the same thing. The statue of limitations of two years had run out. The date for determining this was based on the day of his illegal admission to the hospital, not on the date of his release.

Joe was voluntarily readmitted to the State Hospital on April 2, 1971, and would stay until June 4, 1971. On April 4, 1971, the MMPI, Quick Test was given to Joe by Dr. R., Clinical Psychologist at the hospital. The report in full stated:

"REPORT OF ROUTINE PSYCHOLOGICAL SCREENING

"Patient: Soukup, Joseph
"Age: 28
"Procedures: MMPI, Quick Test

"Date: April 4, 1971

"Admission: April 2, 1971

"The results of intellectual screening suggest Average intelligence. However, it is noted that Mr. Soukup has previously been diagnosed as Borderline Mental Retardation and the validity of this estimate may be questionable. The results of personality screening may be invalid. He may have misunderstood the directions, may have been trying to 'fake bad', or he may have a severe psychiatric disturbance. To the extent the results are valid, they suggest he is aware of and concerned about asocial attitudes and emotional impulse but is unable to control them. He seems somewhat tense and restless and mildly depressed or pessimistic. He has a some-what above average number of physical complaints and is likely concerned about bodily functions and physical health. He may be touchy, overly responsive to the opinions of others, and inclined to blame others for his own difficulties. He may have feelings of unreality, bizarre confused thinking and conduct, and strange attitudes and false beliefs."

On April 5, 1971, Caseworker C. N. wrote the following re-admission note: "Mr. Soukup returned to the Lincoln Regional Center after living in Omaha for about two years. He states that his existence was very marginal during these two years and he has no desire to return to society. He threatens that if he is not allowed to stay in the hospital he will 'not see his twenty-ninth birth-day.' He feels that the state should feel an obligation to keep him here since they have robbed him of so many years already. (He states he has spent 18 of his 28 years in state institutions.)

"Plans for the future may be somewhat difficult since Mr. Soukup does not want to leave the hospital, has no motivation to get or keep a job, and does not want vocational training of any type."

On April 9, 1971, Dr. R. completed the following:

"MENTAL STATUS EXAMINATION

"GENERAL APPEARANCE AND ATTITUDE: Mr. Soukup is a tall, thin, undernourished man appearing about his stated age of 28. He was pleasant and cooperative during the examination. Behavior and appearance in the interview were unremarkable.

"STREAM OF MENTAL ACTIVITY: Mr. Soukup's speech was relatively spontaneous and his vocabulary and use of language was unremarkable. He was somewhat circumstantial at times, but he was generally relevant, coherent, and able to reach goal ideas. Associations were intact.

"MOOD AND AFFECT: His mood was one of mild depression and resentment. While he reports some suicidal ideation in recent months, there is no evidence of suicidal risk at the present time.

"MENTAL CONTENT: There was no evidence of any hallucinations, delusions, or ideas of reference. Mr. Soukup has many resentments about his early life and the time he has spent in institutions. He feels that since he was detained in the hospital without legal basis for a number of years, the hospital now "owes" him a place to stay and avoid pressures of outside living. He appears exceedingly dependent and passive-aggressive. He indicates that he is willing to find employment and leave the hospital in the near future if the staff insists, but indicates this is only because he agreed to this when he was admitted.

"SENSORIUM AND MENTAL CAPACITY: Mr. Soukup is correctly oriented. His fund of information is quite good and his memory, intellectual control, ability to calculations, etc. are unremarkable. He is able to conceptualize and think abstractly, although some of his responses are inconsistent with the previous diagnosis of borderline mental retardation, and in fact, when one looks at the psychological report on which that diagnosis had been based, the examiner had stated that the intellectual testing at that time was probably a minimal estimate of Mr. Soukup's ability given his mental state at that time. It was hypothesized at that time that he had average intelligence.

"INSIGHT AND JUDGEMENT: Mr. Soukup holds doggedly to the positions outlined above and lacks flexibility in evaluating his circumstances. His insight must be seen as limited. His judgment has often been poor, but he seems capable of learning better self-direction.

"IMPRESSION: Inadequate personality."

This examination was also signed by C. R., M.D., Psychiatrist.

The WAIS was administered to Joe on April 13, 1971, by S. S., Associate Psychologist, under the supervision of V. F., Ph.D., Director of Psychology, with the following results:

"Results: Mr. Soukup functioned in the Average Range of intelligence (Full Scale IQ 91). This would seem, in view of his variations in mood and degree of cooperativeness, to be a minimal estimate. He can undoubtedly function somewhat higher when his mood changes are not interfering. Mr. Soukup was quite erratic both within and between the various subtests. His best scores were on general information, abstract reasoning, a timed visual-motor task which also involves some abstract reasoning, and differentiating essential from unessential detail. His worst score were [sic] on a monotonous type of visual-motor task, social judgment and common sense, and the interpretation of social situations."

A referral note to the Behavior Modification Program at the Center was dated April 9, 1971. It listed his 1969 diagnosis as inadequate personality and borderline mental retardation. Employment history was stated, "Has worked as a janitor, dishwasher, busboy, and running errands on the hospital grounds. Has only had short time employment. It has also been reported that he has worked as a manager in flop houses. He has been in an institution for 18 years. He has been receiving welfare."

The document also gave a social history summary, "He has had hullucinations [sic] and 'magical thinking'. Prior to 1965, he had seizures. He was at Lincoln Regional Center illegally and feels society owes him for such action. This particular incident happened when he was transferred from the boys' training school at the age of 21 (*actually occurred at age twelve*). He has made suicidal threats. He does not want to leave the hospital and will make such threats when plans for a discharge are made.

"When he was 5 he was removed from his home due to lack of parental supervision. Mother was an alcoholic and died of cancer in 1963 and was reported to be quite cruel to him. His father was also quite hostile. He is also dead. He had a sister in Omaha who had shown much interest and concern, but recently has not. His brother-in-law refuses to have him in the home. He feels that his sister has had more opportunity than he.

"Ward Behavior: He is very boastful. He does well in his work and takes pride in this. He has been a very good janitor.

"Reinforcers for his behavior modification program were listed as:

"1. One to one relationship

"2. Janitorial work

"3. Time with Mrs. K.

"4. Tour guide

"5. 'Highlights' worker

"Joe's psychriatrist [sic] was listed as Dr. R."

On April 20, 1971, Caseworker C. N. noted, "Transfer Note: On April 19, 1971 Mr. Soukup was transferred to R-1 so he could be involved in the Behavior Modification Program. It was thought that since he is so institutionalized it would be good for him to not have it so easy here in the hospital but would rather have to work for his privileges as he will have to when he lives in society."

On May 7, 1971, E. W. writes, "Joseph was transferred to the Token Economy program on April 19, 1971. The immediate goals determined at that time were 1) employment, and 2) social interaction with peers, particularly within the community. The ultimate goal was community living and employment.

"The patient progressed to Level II on April 25, 1971. He has been doing well on the ward and has made a definite schedule for himself as to when he will be on Level III and be discharged from the hospital.

"At this time Joseph has had interviews for employment as a janitor with K & C Industries. If he is definitely excepted for this job, he will be earning $2.00 an hour and will probably be located in Grand Island. These are only tentative plans at this time and nothing definite has been arranged concerning his employment."

On June 4, 1971, Joe was discharged from the hospital. Dr. K. stated, "This 28 year old, single, Catholic, white male was originally admitted to the Lincoln State Hospital on March 15, 1957, having been transferred from the boys' [sic] Training School in Kearney, Nebraska. He has been in and out of the hospital several times. Mr. Soukup was readmitted to the Lincoln Regional Center on April 2, 1971 as a voluntary commitment. His diagnosis is Inadequate Personality. Upon admission the patient was slightly depressed. There was no evidence of psychotic thinking or behavior. The patient was first treated in AD Bldg. And on April 19, 1971 he was transferred to R-4. Since being in R Bldg. Mr. Soukup has usually been cooperative and pleasant. He helped with the ward work. He did not show any delusions or hallucinations. He was oriented in all three spheres and his memory was satisfactory. His IQ was 91. His physical condition was good. During his stay in the hospital this time, Mr. Soukup was not on medication. On June 4, 1971 the patient was discharged. He will live in Central Hotel, 13th and O Street, Lincoln, Nebraska."

Caseworker I, E. W. documented the discharge. "Joe was placed on a discharge status on June 4, 1971. . . . Joe did not have a job upon his release. He was previously employed by Mr. W. at the Lincoln Housing Authority as a janitor but he quit this job, although he stated that he was just temporarily laid off and would resume the work again after school was out. Also, Joe stated that he was not paid for any of the work he had completed. However, Mr. W. stated that he was given a check for $15.60 and would be receiving another check on this date. When Joe was confronted with what Mr. W. had said, he said that this was true but he had to pay for previous debts and therefore had no money. The check he received on this date will be sufficient to cover expenses until he finds employment.

"Joe was placed on discharge status as he was not benefiting from psychiatric care and he was using the hospital as a home rather than a place for treatment. He was becoming quite comfortable and institutionalized and it was felt that he should be out living in the community as he was capable to do so."

E. W. made the following note on June 17, 1971, "Jo [sic] contacted me on this date inquiring about his Social Security checks which have not arrived.

"Joe is staying with a friend at 323 F Street, temporarily. This is his third address since his discharge.

"At the present time, Joe is working for Manpower and has been unable to find full time employment. He is somewhat discouraged but feels he 'can make it on his own power'. On June 23, 1971 again called looking for his check."

In a document dated September 1, 1971, vocational rehabilitation counselor R. R. offered the following evaluation: "The client appears to be extremely dependent and passive aggressive and has resentments about his early life, also the time spent in institutions. He lacks flexibility in evaluating situations and his judgments are awkward and poor. His feeling and attitudes about his ability and what people are doing for him interferes with any type of vocational assistance he can derive from association with the program. When attempting to do something on his own he may become very upset and belligerent when suggestions and criticisms are given. Academically he functions at the very low level as he has only completed the 7th grade. He does well in his work and takes pride in what he is doing[.] He is generally responsible and dependable in coming to work and working at his assigned tasks. On the WAIS he has a FSIQ of 91. Joseph is very boastful about his ability and the things he is able to accomplish in such a way he does not make good relationships for social interactions with his peers and community contacts. He has been associated with institutions for so long his reactions are generally those related to a hospital routine. Programs which are to be developed will require funding as client has no source of income. The client has sufficient skills in the janitorial area to not require further training." Counseling and guidance were suggested followed by grounds placement, community placement, discharge and follow-up.

The last document in the thirty-two pages of records Joe has from his years at the State Hospital is a November 2, 1971, Out-Patient Progress Note dictated by Caseworker E. W. It states, "Joe contacted this worker on 11-1-71. He continues to be employed on a part-time basis and live with friends. He states that he has adjusted satisfactorily in the community but he appears to be quite reluctant concerning breaking off his dependency upon the hospital although he has been discharged. D. P. will be the contact person as of this date."

Joe's Life After the State Hospital

AFTER leaving the State Hospital, Joe sought justice, approaching the Nebraska Civil Liberties Union, Legal Aid, and even the State Hospital. He approached private attorneys to handle his case for a percentage of the settlement. No one would take his case.

Joe wrote President Jimmy Carter twice but received no answer. He also wrote Congressional Representative Virginia Smith and felt some gratitude when she at least took the time to write back that she was unable to help him.

Joe eventually moved to Grand Island, Nebraska, renting a small apartment and tried to live on monthly SSI. Because his feet had been damaged by years of poor shoes (no one donates size 17 shoes to the state and no special shoes were ordered for Joe), he was only able to do limited jobs such as shoveling snow for a little extra money.

Things Change

If Joe did not love reading the newspaper, his case may have never developed. He would go to the *Grand Island Daily Independent* to pick up a copy of the local paper. Billy Winter, whose desk was near the front of the newspaper office, would visit with Joe and became interested in his story. She suggested the story to reporter Bill Roberts, who interviewed Joe and wrote the first article. The article posed a simple question, "Were his rights violated?" It outlined Joe's effort to seek relief and discussed many of the "Catch-22s" of his case. Betsey Berger, an attorney for DPI, contacted by the newspaper, stated Joe could have access to his records if he had been committed by a mental health board hearing or a court order. Since Joe was never committed, the very point of his case, he could have no access. The statute of limitations precluded obtaining a court order.

Joe hoped the article might reach "the right person" who could answer his questions. The article ended with a quote from Joe: "I look at it this way. If I don't have any rights, neither does anybody else." The article appeared in the evening edition on Saturday, October 29, 1977.

The Saturday paper is the least read of the week so it was very fortunate that Grand Island State Senator Ralph Kelly read the article, became interested in Joe and invited him to his office to discuss his case. Senator Kelly contacted local attorney Jim Livingston who agreed to take his case. After researching available records, Senator Kelly said, "Joe Soukup appears to me to be the result of an incompetent government social welfare system."

In August 1978, Judge Samuel Van Pelt heard arguments in Lincoln's district court. Joe sought copies of his hospital records for a possible $5 million dollar lawsuit if his rights were violated. Livingston argued the records were necessary to determine if there was a cause to file suit. Assistant State Attorney General Kirk Brown, representing the state, argued Joe should first file suit and then obtain the records by court order. Joe was questioned on the witness stand about his case by his attorney Jim Livingston:

Question: "At the time of each transfer between institutions were there any official hearings?"
Joe: "Not to my knowledge."
Question: "Was there every any explanation of the reason you were being transferred?"
Joe: "Not to my knowledge."
Question: "During this time, did you have a guardian or conservator of any kind?"
Joe: "Not to my knowledge."
Question: "Have you ever been able to look at or see the records of your institutionalization?"
Joe: "No, I have not."

Van Pelt ruled against Joe, citing the Statute of Limitations.

In January 1979, Joe took his case to the Nebraska Unicameral with a $1.25 million claim alleging violation of this constitutional and human rights. His case was heard by the Legislative Claims Board in February. On March 5, 1979, the Lincoln Star newspaper published a column by Staff Writer Patty Beutler. In the article Joe's history was reviewed and Lincoln Regional Center (formerly the State Hospital) psychiatrist Klaus Hartmann stated Joe had not signed a voluntary commitment form when he turned twenty-one. The omission was probably an "administrative oversight" involving no malevolence.

"No one would make an attempt to keep a person illegally," he said. Record-keeping now is much more "refined."

The article also went on to point out that the miscellaneous claims include general areas for which there are no specific appropriations from the Legislature, but for which the State may feel a moral obligation to award damages even if the two-year statute of limitations has run out. Jim Livingston asked the Claims Board to subpoena Joe's records, but the Attorney General rendered an opinion that the Claims Board lacked the statutory right to do so. Livingston said, "The law is kind of a built-in veil for the State of Nebraska. It's got a Catch-22 throughout." Jill Nagy, attorney for DPI, said attorneys have access to information in their clients' records, as do patients, unless the staff treatment team decides it is better from a "medical standpoint" to keep the information from the patient. Joe and his attorney wanted more than just access, they wanted copies of the documents. And the Claims Board would not make a decision on Joe's case without the records to validate his situation.

On March 7, 1979, Legislative Bill 580 had its first reading before the Unicameral. It read, "Section I. The following claims against the state, filed with and submitted without recommendation by the State Claims Board, are hereby disapproved: DESCRIPTION Claim No. 103, against the Department of Public Institutions, pay to Joseph James Soukup, c/o James D. Livingston, (Attorney), P.O. Box 878, Grand Island, Nebraska, 68801, out of the General Fund $1,250,000.00."

On March 19, 1979, the *Legislative Journal* published Resolution 29 which had been approved by a vote of 26-9. It read:

"RESOLUTION

"Legislative Resolution 29.

"Introduced by Business and Labor Committee: Maresh, 32nd District, Chairman; Brennan, 9th District; Simon, 31st District; Landis, 46th District; Fitzgerald, 14th District; DeCamp, 40th District.

"WHEREAS, Joseph James Soukop of Grand Island has submitted a claim of $1,250,000 to the Eighty-Sixth Legislature, First Session, and said claim has been referred to the Business and Labor Committee for public hearing and recommendations; and

"WHEREAS, the claimant alleges that on several occasions his constitutional rights to due process were violated; and that statutory procedures were not complied with by the State of Nebraska; and that his physical and psychological treatments while under the care of the State of Nebraska was [sic] inadequate, improper, insufficient and negligent resulting in permanent physical and psychological injury; and

"WHEREAS, essential records and other important information have not been gathered for a full investigation and review of the claim submitted and the claimant's allegations; and

"WHEREAS, the action denying or granting this claim may set a course of precedent for the State and the denying or granting of this claim absent through investigation of the claimant's allegation, claimant's records, and other relevant information may be premature without substantial basis.

"NOW, THEREFORE, BE IT RESOLVED BY THE MEMBERS OF THE EIGHTY-SIXTH LEGISLATURE OF THE STATE OF NEBRASKA, FIRST SESSION:

"1. That the Executive Board create a select committee composed of the members of the Business and Labor Committee, to conduct a special investigation with the powers to subpoena all pertinent records and documents and obtain other information by testimony and investigation involving the claim of Joseph James Soukop.

"2. That the committee recommend the granting or denying of this claim to the Legislature after reviewing the results of the investigation.

Throughout the next three-year battle, the Legislature would kick this issue from board to board. Four tactics are familiar to any bureaucrat faced with "doing the right thing." Those are:

1. "If we do it, we'll set precedent."
2. "If we do it, we open ourselves to a lawsuit."
3. "We'll study the situation."
4. "It's not an investigation; we're 'revisiting' the situation."

In Joe's case, he believes the tactic used was to divert attention from the "real issue," his being held illegally at the State Hospital. The state acknowledged their mistake but tried to make the point that it was "just a technicality" since Joe would have been committed "anyway." The "blame -the-victim" approach is one way to mitigate others actions. They were "just doing what they would have done anyway," that is, providing treatment for a patient who needed care. One of the problems with this argument is that we can never know who Joe would have been had he not spent fourteen years of his first twenty-four in an institution. Well-meaning folks wanted to rehabilitate him, but was he habilitated in the first place?

Joe's attorneys, Jim Livingston and Bill Riley, testified before a variety of Legislative committees, attempting to convince someone to take responsibility for the injustice that was done to Joe by the state. After reviewing Joe's history, Mr. Livingston made several important points:

1. Joe's original transfer to the State Hospital in 1960 was without his appearance before any board or hearing; no due process.

2. The transfer order stated he be held until he obtained the age of twenty-one years.

3. In 1964 Joe celebrated his twenty-first birthday at the Lincoln State Hospital and was not released or committed; no due process.

Mr. Livingston went on to say, ". . . it happened a long time age, that this happened in the 1950s, in the 1960s and then in the 1970s. Why should we address it now? I believe the responsibility of government in the State of Nebraska and government anywhere is to be responsible to its citizens and to correct wrongs which have been done, among other duties. The fact that it happened some time ago should not reflect of the fact that it did happen to this gentleman. That this person was taken into the arms of the State of Nebraska and spent most of his formative years in the arms of the State of Nebraska and came out, as we will tell you, in the situation he is now in. The second item is and it may be said that to grant Joe Soukup's claim would set a precedent or a bad precedent, I suppose, for the State of Nebraska. I don't feel it's a bad precedent at any time to correct a wrong that has been done or to make reparations for a wrong that has been done. This country was founded on precedent that if legislators did not establish precedent, we wouldn't be where we are today in numerous fields. The philosophy that the king can do no wrong was overturned when, I think, our forefathers left the mother country and became 'can do wrong' and 'has done wrong.' And the criminal laws in the State of Nebraska when an individual commits a crime against the State of Nebraska, it's against the people of the State of Nebraska. . . . If you violate the law and the rights of the people of Nebraska, you can be punished in numerous ways for numerous periods of time. Well, we have the reverse here with Joseph Soukup. The people of Nebraska have violated the rights of Joseph Soukup. I would put forth to you that an injustice which occurs anywhere is a threat to justice everywhere. Today I bring before you an injustice which has occurred to this gentleman."

In response to a question from Senator Maresh regarding the actions of the doctors and other staff who were responsible for Joe's being given an experimental drug, LSD, Mr. Livingston responded, "I do not think they were acting within the law at that time. I think it was condoned at that time by the head of your institution evidently that they were conducting experiments with drugs for private drug firms and getting paid by those drug firms for doing that. The individual who kept Joe Soukup after he was twenty-one years old, that is the system that kept him. I think it's the system that was run by the State of Nebraska. The ultimate responsibility goes to the doctor of this wing of the institution to the state hospital to the head of what was then the Board of Control to the State Legislature."

Senator Wiitala questioned Joe's lawyers about their fees. Repeatedly, they had to deny that they were engaged by Joe on a contingency basis. Their expenses were for investigation of Joe's history alone and for the cost of a doctor's examination of his feet and a vocational rehabilitation evaluation. Any reimbursement for these expenses would be the decision of the administrator of the trust fund.

Both attorneys were asked, "Did Joe ever do anything wrong?" Both responded to the negative and Bill Riley went on to say, ". . . I have to quickly add even if he had done anything wrong, I can't. . . there is no evidence that would indicate he should be confined and treated the way he was during this period of time."

Joe attended all the hearings but declined to give testimony. It was not easy hearing and re-hearing the details of his youth and his time in institutions. It seemed to Joe the senators continued to try to find fault in his actions or his lawyers' actions as a means of taking the heat off the basic fact of the case: Joe was held without legal grounds in the Lincoln State Hospital.

On March 10, 1981, Joe's request, LB 548, finally reached floor debate in the State Legislature. Senator Richard Maresh discussed a number of claims for state monies. In regard to Joe he stated, "The next one is the Joseph H. Soukup Trust Fund. The Claims Board allowed this claim and they didn't have any recommendation for the amount. It came to us and we didn't know what to do with it, and I asked for an Attorney General's opinion and he decided it was in the wrong. . . with the wrong Board, that it should not be handled by this Claims Board, so we sent it back to the Claims Board and they again allowed it without any amount and this time we decided to set up a trust fund of $30,000, and figuring thirteen percent interest, this would bring in to Mr. Soukup about $337 a month in addition to his $220 a month Social Security, we figured this would be probably a reasonable amount for him to live on, so this is the amount we recommended to the Legislature to be allowed. This money will be invested with the Investment Council and we hope that they can make monthly payments to Mr. Soukup. This will be for the duration of this lifetime, and after his death, $30,000 goes back to the general fund."

Senators John DeCamp and Howard Peterson then moved to amend the committee recommendations, striking $30,000, and inserting $50,000. Senator DeCamp then made the following statement. "Mr. President and members of the Legislature, the Joe Soukup story has been told and retold, heard and reheard so many times that I do not want to expend any significant amount of time on it. Suffice it to say that in all the settlements and discussions on this matter the minimum amounts we always talked about were either eighty or one hundred thousand, something like that. Therefore, to make it $50,000 does not seem even slightly unreasonable and maybe not reasonable enough. But it is an acknowledgement that here was a person that, by every standard there is, we did a lot of damage to him as a state, and I think we have to establish the precedent that we have to make up for these errors whether it be the LSD testing he was used for as a guinea pig, whether it be the damage to his feet that was caused, whether it be the illegal holding of him for any number of years after he should have been released, so on and so forth. As I say, I don't want to spend two hours or an hour reviewing the case because I think every member has had ample opportunity to review it. Do remember this, that in the past the Claims Board simply rejected it. When they finally had the facts and realized. . . and realized that we were serious, that there was something that needed to be corrected, the Claims Board finally came around and they said, yes, damages should be paid, something should be done, and they simply left up to the Legislature the amount. Now I am suggesting $50,000 is a reasonable amount."

Senator Tom Vickers then rose in opposition, voicing objections that had arisen over the years. He stated, ". . . I would remind the body that there was an Attorney General's Opinion dated April the 9th in reply to Senator Maresh in this Joe Soukup claim matter, and the Attorney General's Opinion was that it is probably unconstitutional for the Legislature to pay Mr. Soukup through the miscellaneous claim procedure, and to be specific about it say, and I quote from the Attorney General's Opinion, 'Payment of Mr. Soukup's miscellaneous claim would probably violate Article III, Section 18, Article I, Section 16, or the Nebraska Constitution.' Now it is without a doubt that Mr. Soukup had some bad things happen to him, but it was my contention in the committee that the procedure should have been followed through the court procedure. I think the attorneys for Mr. Soukup are using us, leaning on our sensitivities, if you will, on our conscience, and I am sure the state did something that might have been bad, I don't know. I am not sure of it. . . I shouldn't say it that way, I am not sure, I don't know. That's been alleged, and if that is the case then I think the courts would probably award a generous payment. But I think we are being asked to be judge and jury in this manner [probably meant "matter" – Ed.] and that bothers me. I think the court system in this nation is set up to answer these types of questions. I don't think the legislative body is the one to set up to do it."

Then Senator Nichols added his views. "Here we go again. What happens when anybody else has a claim? They go through the courts. Why hasn't this gone through the courts? Probably because they don't think they can win. Now we all have a bleeding heart for this poor man and it is pitiful. It's too bad, but let's look at the other side just a minute. Has he had any benefits from the state? Did he ever eat on the state? Did they ever pay for his lodging and clothing, food? You bet. And here we are brought in because the committee says, let's pay him a figure that they pull out of the hat, and Senator DeCamp is pulling a different figure out of the hat. If he really has the money coming, we are way under the money. If he doesn't have any coming, we are over the money, and we are making a decision here, just plunk out a bunch of cash, just plunk out a piece of money. And this doesn't seem reasonable for a body like this to act that way. I think we are more responsible than to be either softhearted or hardhearted just as our whims seems to guide us."

Senator Peterson responded to Mr. Vickers by reviewing the history of the claim, including its three-year history at Legislative committee level, and stated, "Apparently the Claims Court this last year voted two to one to recommend to this body that a claim be allowed, then it was returned again to the Claims Court again this year. They just recently voted to allow it again two to one and said the amount ought to be set by the Legislature. I would just like to read you a letter that I received from Joe Soukup. Bear in mind this is a letter from a guy who supposedly has lost all his marbles, a fellow who was in the institution out here, I think abused, and really as John [DeCamp] indicated was used as a guinea pig. This is what he says: 'First, what options do I have after you Senators get through with my claim? Senator Peterson, I do not want further education or job training through the state. The state has already ruined my life enough. If I want any of them, it will be my choice. My claim is for a money amount. That is what I want. The state had me for fifteen years plus years. For the most part they didn't follow through on their obligation as my guardian. Now that I am out here I am involved with the state. As one of your constituents it is an obligation for me to inform you just how I feel. Since my future rides on how this situation comes out, I am trying to work as close as I can with you.

"'I want you to stay on top of my claim. The reason why I am suggesting $50,000 rather than $30,000, this man gets $220 a month and it just seems to me in today's economy if you invest $50,000, you are going to have to hustle to get enough for him to live on even at that kind of figure.'"

Senator Kahle was also concerned about setting precedent and opening the door to ". . . many thousand people we have had in our institutions since the beginning of Nebraska's statehood." He also said, "I just doubt if you will find anybody that's been in an institution that thinks they haven't been abused in one way or another, and I don't know if we know whether Joe Soukup was abused when he, for instance, when he was out at Kearney. He says he was. But perhaps the treatment that was given at that time was proven to be wrong and there is nothing to say that the treatment that we are giving the people in our institutions today is going to be right ten years from now or twenty years from now. . . . I just wonder too . . . I understood there are lawyer fees involved at one time in this case when they were asking for the larger sum. . . . if we pay any amount or set up any kind of trust, will we be obligated for those lawyer fees?"

Senator DeCamp closed his amendment with the following statement, "Mr. President, I am thrown into a state of stupor at some of the statements. Here, you poor dumb clod, go to court, except we have laws that say, no, you have to go through the claim system. Finally he uses the system, he follows the system, he goes to the Claims Court, he gets approval. Now you say, hey, dummy, go to court. The court said, go through the claim system. How much Catch-22 do you want to play with people's lives? Now this bad guy, let me tell you his crime. Let me tell you Joe Soukup's crimes so you know why we locked him up for twenty years. Joe Soukup created the unforgivable crime of being a neglected seven-year-old kid. Yeah, can you imagine anything so heinous, so evil? Joe Soukup was a neglected seven-year-old kid who got into the system and once in the system he was used for LSD experiments. He was kept contained and locked up because we shoved him from one thing to another, from one institution to another because we didn't want to take care of him, we didn't know what to do with him. As a result of the Joe Soukup study, we have changed law after law after law in this state. So if it has done nothing else, it has been one heck of a laboratory to examine our system, to repudiate what Senator Kahle just said, we've got no business looking into this. No business, my derriere, it is exactly our business to see how our systems function, see how our institutions function. If there is any forgotten institution, it is our mental and penal institutions. They are the ones we don't want to look at. They are the ones we don't want to examine. If there is something wrong, golly, we want to cover it up. We have learned one heck of a lot out of the Soukup cases. He has followed the system all the way and about those attorney's fees, there is something called *pro bono*. It means lawyers, whoever, who believe that wrong has been done and simply donate their time. To any of those, including my good friend Senator Vickers, would you let us lock you up and stick LSD into you for twenty years for $50,000? I doubt it."

The amendment to raise the recommended amount from $30,000 to $50,000 was then passed with a vote of twenty-five ayes and twenty-two nays. The bill to establish a trust fund for Joe then passed with a vote of twenty-six ayes and eleven nays.

Views expressed by Nebraska senators were an interesting reflection of their values. One of the most interesting is the observation by Senator Nichols which deals with the food and lodging Joe received while being held illegally at the State Hospital! What a perk: institution food, a single bed in a dorm with sixty others, and clothing and shoes that didn't fit! What's next? Should Joe be sent a bill for his room and board at the State

Hospital? All this while admitting Joe was held without legal commitment!

Another tactic that always is useful: Blame the lawyers! Were they bleeding hearts or money-grubbers or both? Or should the legislature follow the dictate of their own lawyer, the attorney general? All these maneuvers were ways to avoid taking responsibility for the state's actions.

If Joe's stay at the State Hospital was not legal, then Joe's behavior at the hospital, his room and board, even his lawyer's motivations, are irrelevant. Like the "fruit of the poisonous tree," once the illegal act is established, all that follows is immaterial.

Luckily, Senator DeCamp was willing to get up off his "derriere" and make the point of legislative responsibility not only for Joe but for anyone in a state institution. Joe received a letter dated August 17, 1981, from Donald G. Erway, Acting State Risk Manager for the State Claims Board. The letter informed him that pursuant to L.B. 548 which became effective on August 30, 1981, Joe would be receiving a check each month. On October 26, 1981, Joe finally received a check from the State of Nebraska for $788.29. The letter also stated, "In order for you to have accurate records of all payments received, we would be happy to mail the checks to your bank for deposit. Would you please advise us of the name and address of the bank where you have a checking account and your account number." Was this really a concern for Joe's benefit or the state's attempt to control his access to the actual checks? The tone of the "request" appears more a command than an offer and would allow the state to never be open to criticism if a check were lost.

Others' Response to Joe

JOE'S sister Patricia was contacted to comment on Joe's life. She writes:
"I will do what I can to assist you with your book.

"As a child, my memories are few and far between. When quite small, a happy experience when we got our 1st T.V. set. The whole family was excited, as Dad set it up for us to view. Those days, there were only a few times per day that <u>any</u> thing was on, at all. I remember a happy family event; a birthday or such. Many people, much laughter. I remember mom's fudge which seemed to take hrs. to make. I remember her favorite songs. A radio atop the refrig. I used to stand on a chair by the refrig and listen and sing along to her favorites. One was 'Your Cheating Heart'. As she cooked supper I sang to her. She was a protective mother - one day a neighbor man made an advance, verbally to me and she came unglued at him, when I told her what had occurred. (than a lapse of memory!) We were alone with mom. I <u>don't ever remember</u> them fighting! Strange isn't it??!?

"Mom took to alcohol. Joe came home late a lot and got a whipping with the belt. This bothered me a lot. Mom took ill. She was in bed a lot. I cooked canned veg to feed us. It was all I could do - so young. How long she layed there - I know not! One day, dad came over and knew immediately she was in trouble. He got her to the Hosp. But within a week she was dead.

"My dad was the greatest!! He loved to take pictures. We had boxesfuls. Where they went, we will never know. Dad had another family he use to visit them and take us with. I remember my other brothers tossing me around in play. Dad worked nites as an airport driver or cab. We were left alone, until one nite - - - someone tried to brake in. I'll never know if someone reported it or if Dad, himself decided it was time to get help. So he wouldn't have to worry about us.

"None-the-less, soon we were put into a place called Riverview Home, a Hell hole. I felt like I was in a child's reformatory. Joe was abused even worse. He used to tell Dad that they beat him in the basement with a rubber hose. Not sure if Dad believed him. Years late I heard they closed down Riverview home, and on the news, they stated that kids were beat with rubber hoses because they didn't leave the usual marks. I was in SHOCK!!!!!

"Dad did his best to get us out. I was 1st. I went to St. James orphanage. Joe came for a short time but kept running away and they sent him on to Kearney Reform. It was years before I know anything of him (at Lincoln Mental Hosp).

"Dad visited me weekly with <u>Big</u> Bags of fruit and candies. I was the most popular girl in the orphanage. Than dad took to cancer but still came until it became too much. A <u>big</u> bandage covered ½ of his face, in the end. I asked him if it hurt and he responded - "more than you'll ever know." Soon he stopped coming and eventually died. But I was elated when I heard he died with a rosary in his hands. I knew he made his piece with God.

"As for Joe and I as kids, I remember playing cowboys etc with him. Not a lot of memories of Joe. Maybe he had his own friends. I remember how happy we were when a certain uncle came over and gave us each a quarter. It bought a <u>Lot</u> of penny candy back than. At the store across the street.

"I went to the orphanage around 8 yrs old. I was much happier there than a Riverview home. I was there per-say until High School - than to the Good Shepard Home. Yes, I missed Joe in our separation. He was a cute blonde-head boy. When I finally met him years later, I was shocked at the change in his appearance. He was huge and not at all as I remember him.

"We did not know our grandparents. I'm sure we met them. But after our being put away, <u>No One</u> kept in touch with us. I see Joe at X-mas and we try to plan a summer get together. We have grown closer than ever. He calls on a regular basis. It has taken time for this growth. (Picture someone telling you that I am your sister.) These things take time.

"I think Joe has come a long way. He does not completely fit into society as easy as I feel I have. But, he has not had the blessings and opportunities than I have had either. I am so proud of Him in his struggle to pursue that state, as He did. He suffered so much before his claim. Had he not been awarded a settlement, he would not be alive today.

"In all I wrote - I think I have answered many of your questions. (Except) - Joe tries to contact certain family. Bless him! I find it a bit harder. They didn't give a dam about us, as lonely children. Why should I need them now! I too, tried to contact a few when I first attained my freedom. I heard from one aunt that she didn't keep in touch with us because she was afraid we might beg to come live with her and they couldn't keep us - so it was easier to let us be orphaned. That was all I needed to hear!!! My hunt for family was over!! Apparently they all felt the same way!!

"I am divorced, but have 2 lovely daughters and 2 adorable grandchildren. That is all the family I need, along with Joe. But for the record, it is a difficult life for people like Joe and myself. We are doing the best we can. But, having no family to pattern our life after, we create it as we go along. <u>We</u> make the <u>best</u> survivors. But, yet walk in fear, every step we take. I had a sad childhood, but not the hell my brother went thru. But just as I, he is a surviver!!

"I hope I have given you some info into our life. Please excuse my rough writing and errors. But I felt I should get this off to you as soon as I can.

"Sincerely,
"Patricia Thompson"

Joe frequently speaks for classes at Southeast Community College in the Human Services Program. He is committed to telling his story to future workers in the field of behavioral health so that individuals never forget that patients and clients are real human beings. Here are some of the student comments after a recent presentation of Joe's:

David Orbits writes: "Probably the thing I took away from it was never give up. What I mean is what Joe went through from birth to now is inspirational, he came through so much adversity and survived some terrible things."

Kiley Epp comments: "What struck me the most about Joe was his ability to speak to classes about his situation. It's amazing to hear his story and see that he is able to do everything on his own, something that the State could not see for all those years. He is a true survivor, such a remarkable story!"

Megan Beeck writes: "The thing that struck a cord [sic] with me about Joe is that this sort of thing could have happened to any one of us born in that era without anyone to look after us." Joe feels the same thing could happen to someone today.

Jennifer Gale said: "Joe seems to be a fascinating man . . . just because he was an orphan and they didn't have anywhere else to put him, that they would put him in an institution. He has a good spirit for going through so much electro shock therapy. I think his face shows a lot. He looks very worn out like he's been though a lot in his lifetime. At the same time he keeps a smile and seems on the positive side. He reminds me of Victor Frankl's existentintail [sic] theory. Frankl survived the Nazi war camps and kept a positive outlook. That's how Joe is."

Kasi O'Keefe stated: "He grew up a lonely man, but was 'stoked' to visit classes and share his story. At the same time he didn't want people to feel sorry for him. But I did. I learned that my life isn't hard and I take simple things for granted."

Michaela Biddle shared: "From Joe I learned how important it is to know your clients, to be involved with your clients and to be a voice for your clients. As Human Services students we hold people's very lives in our hands and that responsibility should not be taken lightly or haphazardly."

Jared Ray stated: "I find Joe's situation very disturbing. . . . Lack of placement should never result in commitment to a mental health hospital or incarceration for that matter. Joe has been deprived of his liberty, life, and pursuit of happiness, which are the elements of life granted to every person that absolutely shouldn't be taken away. It goes to show what can happen in a tough situation when an individual has no representation."

Journalist Bill Roberts, who has known Joe from the beginning of his battle with the state, writes about Joe, "I met Joe Soukup in the fall of 1977. I was a reporter for the *Grand Island Daily Independent* newspaper, and a photographer at the paper, Harry Baumert, a friend of mine since our days together at journalism school in Lincoln, suggested Joe might make an interesting story. Harry had met Joe in Lincoln, where Joe used to talk and talk about his childhood growing up as a ward of the state. So Harry and I went to meet Joe. He lived in a crummy second-story apartment in a crummy part of town, everything old, dirty, dilapidated and I recall being a little nervous, maybe even scared, as we walked in.

"I quickly recognized there was nothing to fear from Joe. His personality then was pretty much the same as it is now. He's gentle, kind, caring, and he wouldn't hurt anyone. He's sharp, although not well educated. He is self-effacing to a fault, and will not complain; these may be traits he picked up from spending his formative years in state institutions. When he speaks about his mistreatment, it's almost in a third-person way, focusing on the hypocrisies of the system, not on the injuries that he suffered. He has a down-home, unpretentious manner and he's quick to see humor in situations, and he's especially quick to spot pretentious behavior and make (gentle) fun of it both in himself and others. But he's not sarcastic or meanspirited in the slightest.

"Joe's story was pretty dramatic. He had been orphaned, taken by the state, shuffled around from place to place, and finally turned out at age twenty-six. It was my job to be skeptical and check out his story, but immediately I felt pretty confident he was telling the truth. My first reaction was to see a big opportunity for my career. I was one of the first wave of journalists emerging from college after the Pentagon Papers, Watergate, etc., and I adored the idea of being a bold reformer, righting a wrong for a mistreated person. As I interviewed Joe more and tried to verify his story and write it, that excitement kind of faded, and I don't remember ever getting any sort of professional benefit from the story.

"As I called around various institutions, his story did check out in general outline, although there were a few differing details, I now see in rereading the article after several years. Talking to social workers at the institutions, most of whom seemed genuinely concerned, I got the impression that here was a child who had become a ward of the state and had been forgotten. Overlooked. With nobody looking out for him; no family, friend or attorney. He had simply fallen through the cracks. Eventually somebody at the State Regional Center noticed that he was still there like nothing was wrong. It was a sad, sad story. At that point, there was no verification of Joe's memories of electroshock therapy and drug experimentation: now I realize it was even worse. They not only neglected him, they abused him. The headline for the story asked, 'Were his rights violated?' And the answer is obviously a resounding yes.

"I worked hard on Joe's story, researching for weeks and rewriting it several times. I didn't have deadline pressure; I put the article together when I felt I had all I could reasonably get. Soon after it ran, which was October 29, 1977, I got a call from Jim Livingston, an attorney who's now a judge. I knew him because he served on the school board, which I covered. He basically asked if this Joe Soukup guy was for real, and I said yes. Soon after, he took Joe's case, and that's when Joe truly made progress toward getting his settlement. Also, Ralph Kelly, who represented Grand Island in the state legislature at the time, was a genuine help. Joe always liked Ralph Kelly personally.

"I think I wrote a few more follow-up stories about Joe before I left Grand Island. Joe and I have corresponded ever since. We send each other anniversary cards every October 29th, something I'm sure Joe started, maybe around the 10th anniversary. Over the past several years, with Joe living in Lincoln and me in Omaha, we see each other twice annually when he comes to visit his sister, Pat. This is usually around Christmas and the Fourth of July. I drive over, pick him up, and we hang around together for an hour or three. He always tells me to choose what we'll do. I like to go someplace together, a museum, exhibit, park, etc. and maybe have lunch too. He likes driving around downtown Omaha and seeing where he lived as a child (where the house stood is now a parking lot for Creighton University). He points out where he went to grade school. I guess those memories are sort of bittersweet for him, but he never complains or speaks with resentment.

"Once we came over to my house and he helped me build a cat scratchier. He and I are both poor carpenters, and Joe has sent me tools several times since then, as a gift and a kind of joke. Even with the finest tools in the world I couldn't make a decent cat scratchier. He likes to send gifts because he's such a kind person; I tell him he doesn't need to do it but that I appreciate them and the sentiment.

"The most recent time I saw Joe, I took him to an exhibit of photography at Joslyn Art Museum. It had such a wide range of photographs that, even though I knew he didn't have a strong interest in photograph art, I thought something there might appeal to him. I remember when we walked in the first gallery, the only other person in the room was a museum security guard, and Joe glanced at the pictures on the wall and went right up to her to begin a conversation: How's it going? How about this weather? Do you like your job? It struck me that, for Joe, the most intriguing work in the room was a person. There is nothing Joe cares about more than people. That's really something for a person who people treated so badly."

Joe's Life Today

Kuhl's Restaurant
"Downtown Lincoln Restaurant"
Complete Breakfast, Lunch & Dinner Menus
Breakfast served all day • Fresh Homemade Pies • Carry Out Orders
Mon - Fri 6 AM - 7 PM • Sat 6 AM - 4 PM • Sun 7 AM - 3 PM
1038 O • 476-1311

ALSO known as Joe's home away from home. Each day begins at 6:30 a.m. in a booth in the smoking section. His waitress is Mary. His breakfast order is a standing one, two eggs, toast and coffee. The bill always comes to $3.37. He leaves a tip of eight quarters. Joe has been eating at this community institution for the past fourteen years. It's where he had his Thanksgiving and Christmas dinner. In 2000, when Joe was the victim of a pedestrian/motor vehicle accident, Kuhl's staff worried until they knew Joe was in the hospital and on the mend.

Joe lives in a one-bedroom apartment directly across from the State Capitol and the Governor's Mansion. The building is called "Capital Square" and was built in the 1920s. Joe's "garden level" apartment is on the southeast corner of the building and is always cold in the winter. He had a window air conditioner but had it removed and just allows the basement and cross ventilation to cool his place in the summer. By his own account, he is not the world's tidiest housekeeper; Heloise does not call him for tips.

Joe spends much of his time watching TV. His favorites include forensic programs (*C.S.I.: Crime Scene Investigation*, the *New Detectives*, and the *F.B.I. Files*), sports shows, and reruns of *M.A.S.H.* and *Cheers*. While he still plays solitaire, he lacks the friends to play other card and board games he learned while in the State Hospital. Joe is a long-time Dodgers baseball fan and his commitment has followed them from Ebert's Field in Brooklyn to their current home in L.A. In the past Joe loved to play ping pong. He doesn't know how to swim, never drove a car, but did ride a bike. Joe purchases a monthly bus pass for his transportation needs in Lincoln. On Sundays Lincoln has no public transportation service so he walks anywhere he needs to go.

Joe no longer attends the Catholic Church; "religion is not a building."

That doesn't mean he is not a spiritual person. Joe keeps his beliefs within himself. He uses his own form of the Serenity Prayer, "God, grant me the serenity to accept the things I can and to change the things that I feel need to be changed." He also likes the images of the "Footprints" story, a parable of Jesus taking care of him when needed.

Joe doesn't swear and considers himself a gentleman from the "old school." His favorite movie is *The Ten Commandments* with Charlton Heston and his all-time favorite book is Stephen King's *Green Mile*. Both works reflect a strong sense of spirituality. His favorite song is the hymn, "You'll Never Walk Alone," and his choice for best singer is Elvis Presley. If his story is made into a movie he would like Jim Carey, Robin Williams, or Tom Hanks to portray him.

Joe is in good health generally and hasn't been to see a doctor since his accident. His feet and toes still hurt from years of ill-fitting shoes and the inability to get good fitting shoes currently. With age, he is getting harder of hearing and his near vision is no longer clear. One day, years ago, Joe got disgusted with his ill-fitting dentures and deposited them in a dumpster as he was out walking. He's just done without since then.

Occasionally Joe has been stopped by police officers because he fits the description of someone they are looking for. All he has to do is show them his size 17 AAA feet and he is eliminated as a suspect. In fact, Joe has never been in trouble in all the years since he left the State Hospital, contrary to the prediction of at least one of his doctors.

Joe follows local and national politics and votes in every election. He is always waiting for the polls to open at 8:00 a.m. at the Lincoln Women's Club, the voting station for his district. He tells them they can close the polls after he votes because he's picked the right persons for the job; they stay open anyway!

Joe calls his sister Pat at 9:00 a.m. every other Sunday morning. She lives in Omaha and works for the University of Nebraska at Omaha; she is married and has two grown daughters. She occasionally invites Joe to join her family for a holiday but he prefers to limit the relationship to a telephone one. He doesn't care for her ex-husband, who is still in the picture. Pat, though the younger, still tries to act the "big sister," the one whose opinions rule; and it is hard to shake the "mental patient" legacy even with one's own sister. His opinions are "right" only if they match her own.

Frugal and generous are two adjectives that apply to Joe. For his own needs, he watches his money carefully, grocery shopping at Sam's Club and buying clothing at the O Street thrift stores. He owns four heavy parka coats for walking and waiting for the bus in Nebraska winters. It is still difficult for him to find shoes that fit; "tennis" shoes are about the only option but they usually come in D width rather than the AAA he needs.

In his actions towards others, he is a very generous person; sometimes to the extent that others take advantage of his kind nature. Of the many "loans" he has made to others, none has ever been paid back.

Joe carries an anatomical donation card and has already paid the $300-plus it will cost for Lincoln Memorial Mortuary to transport his body to the Medical Center in Omaha. A card in his wallet instructs authorities to call the funeral home to put this plan into action. No one will be inconvenienced by his death and his donation will help in the education of future doctors.

With each check he gets, trust fund and SSI, Joe buys $30 of "Cash for Life" lottery tickets. These numbers are good for fifteen days; each night, except Sunday, he stays up to watch the 10:00 p.m. news which includes an announcement of the winning numbers. To date he has won only at the $9 level, but it is fun to follow and Joe figures it is money that isn't wasted; the state will use it to treat gamblers. If he didn't buy the tickets, he would spend the same money in other ways. His other major "vice" is $120 monthly for cigarettes, a habit he acquired at the State Hospital.

Joe defines friends as people that live close to you, ones you can do things with. Given these criteria, Joe leads a lonely life. The neighbors he has befriended have taken advantage of his generosity, one running up $700 worth of charges on Joe's phone. Others he asks to coffee suddenly become hungry and are short on cash to pay for the meal. Joe makes acquaintances easily, but lacks the close friends that would make his life more fulfilling. While Joe has the financial means to do more activities, he lacks the companionship that would make those activities rewarding.

At sixty years of age, Joe looks forward to his speaking engagements to discuss his "journey." He frequently speaks for mental health groups and college classes. It takes the audience a while to catch on to Joe's dry wit and willing honesty.

Participants can literally ask him any question and he will give an answer or opinion. He wants these future professionals to not forget the past and to inspire them to be caring for the rights of others in the future. The Nebraska Leadership Academy holds a yearly four-day training to assist consumers and family members who want to impact the mental health system in Nebraska. Joe has attended each year since its inception, frequently speaking about his case and the history of the organization.

It is a sad fact that Joe has no baby pictures, no scrapbook of senior prom programs, athletic awards, chess championship ribbons. His scrapbook is filled with newspaper clippings highlighting his fight with the State of Nebraska for recognition of the wrongs done to him. Joe believes he has accomplished a great deal in the telling of his story. It is his hope that the lessons learned will guarantee the rights of all citizens in the future.